The Complete Motets 17

RECENT RESEARCHES IN MUSIC

A-R Editions publishes seven series of critical editions, spanning the history of Western music, American music, and oral traditions.

RECENT RESEARCHES IN THE MUSIC OF THE MIDDLE AGES AND EARLY RENAISSANCE
Charles M. Atkinson, general editor

RECENT RESEARCHES IN THE MUSIC OF THE RENAISSANCE
James Haar, general editor

RECENT RESEARCHES IN THE MUSIC OF THE BAROQUE ERA
Christoph Wolff, general editor

RECENT RESEARCHES IN THE MUSIC OF THE CLASSICAL ERA
Eugene K. Wolf, general editor

RECENT RESEARCHES IN THE MUSIC OF THE NINETEENTH AND EARLY TWENTIETH CENTURIES
Rufus Hallmark, general editor

RECENT RESEARCHES IN AMERICAN MUSIC
John M. Graziano, general editor

RECENT RESEARCHES IN THE ORAL TRADITIONS OF MUSIC
Philip V. Bohlman, general editor

Each edition in *Recent Researches* is devoted to works by a single composer or to a single genre. The content is chosen for its high quality and historical importance, and each edition includes a substantial introduction and critical report. The music is engraved according to the highest standards of production using the proprietary software MUSE, owned by Music|Notes.™

For information on establishing a standing order to any of our series, or for editorial guidelines on submitting proposals, please contact:

A-R Editions, Inc.
801 Deming Way
Madison, Wisconsin 53717

800 736-0070 (U.S. book orders)
608 836-9000 (phone)
608 831-8200 (fax)
http://www.areditions.com

RECENT RESEARCHES IN THE MUSIC OF THE RENAISSANCE, 115

Orlando di Lasso

The Complete Motets 17

Motets from Printed Anthologies and Manuscripts, 1555–1569

Edited by Peter Bergquist

A-R Editions, Inc.

Madison

A-R Editions, Inc., Madison, Wisconsin 53717
© 1999 by A-R Editions, Inc.

A-R Editions is pleased to support scholars and performers
in their use of *Recent Researches* material for study or performance. Subscribers to any of the *Recent Researches* series,
as well as patrons of subscribing institutions, are invited to
apply for information about our "Copyright Sharing
Policy."

Printed in the United States of America

ISBN 0-89579-416-0
ISSN 0486-123X

⊗ The paper used in this publication meets the minimum
requirements of the American National Standard for
Information Sciences—Permanence of Paper for Printed
Library Materials, ANSI Z39.48-1984.

Contents

Critical Report   175

Abbreviations

Boetticher, *Lasso*	Wolfgang Boetticher. *Orlando di Lasso und seine Zeit.* Kassel: Bärenreiter, 1958.
CM	Orlando di Lasso. *The Complete Motets.* Recent Researches in the Music of the Renaissance. Madison: A-R Editions, 1995–.
KBM5/1	Martin Bente et al. *Bayerische Staatsbibliothek: Katalog der Musikhandschriften. 1. Chorbücher und Handschriften in chorbuch-artiger Notierung.* Kataloge Bayerischer Musiksammlungen, Bd. 5/1. Munich: Henle, 1989.
Leuchtmann, *Leben*	Horst Leuchtmann. *Orlando di Lasso: Sein Leben.* Wiesbaden: Breitkopf und Härtel, 1976.
LV	Horst Leuchtmann. *Lasso-Verzeichnis.* Forthcoming in *SWNR.*
MOM	Orlando di Lasso. *Magnum Opus Musicum.* Munich: N. Henrici, 1604.
RISM	Répertoire international des sources musicales. *Einzeldrucke vor 1800.* Series A/I/5. Kassel: Bärenreiter, 1975; *Receuils imprimés XVIᵉ–XVIIᵉ siècles.* Series B/I. Munich: Henle, 1960.
SW	Orlando di Lasso. *Sämtliche Werke.* Ed. Franz Xaver Haberl and Adolf Sandberger, 21 vols. Leipzig: Breitkopf und Härtel, 1894–1927. Reprint, 1973.
SW2	Orlando di Lasso, *Sämtliche Werke: Zweite, nach den Quellen revi-dierte Auflage.* Ed. Horst Leuchtmann. Wiesbaden: Breitkopf und Härtel, 1968–.
SWNR	Orlando di Lasso. *Sämtliche Werke, neue Reihe.* Ed. Siegfried Hermelink et al., 25 vols. Kassel: Bärenreiter, 1956–95.

General Preface

The aim of the present edition is to publish Orlando di Lasso's motets in a format that will make them more accessible to scholars, students, and performers than they have been in the past, to present a more reliable text of all of the motets than has heretofore been available, and to respect Lasso's own intentions about grouping and context as demonstrated in authoritative editions with which he himself was associated. Since Lasso's motets were all published during or soon after his lifetime, this edition will be based, with only a few exceptions, on the earliest printed sources (some partbooks for a few of these sources do not survive; the missing voice parts will be supplied from other early editions). Lasso's surviving correspondence and his prefaces to many of the books attest that almost all of the first editions of the motets were issued with his involvement and permission. For this edition, motets contained in authoritative manuscripts, primarily the choirbooks from Lasso's own *Hofkapelle,* now held in the Musikabteilung of the Bayerische Staatsbibliothek, will be compared to the printed versions. Other manuscript sources less directly connected with Lasso, if indeed at all, are usually of no value for establishing a text and thus will not be consulted. A limited amount of comparison with printed sources other than first editions may occur, but a full-scale critical examination of all the extant sources is not intended. Most of the motets in this edition will be based on first editions. Wherever possible, a single volume will present motets that are contained in a single source. Limiting the sources considered may occasionally result in omitting a significant variant from a later publication, but the first editions almost always present good texts, and they are more closely associated with Lasso than are reprints, over which he often had less control.

Approximately 120 motets were copied into the surviving choirbooks of Lasso's *Hofkapelle.* Some of these copies are dated earlier, some later, than the first publications. For the sake of consistency this edition will be organized entirely around dates of publication, though earlier dates established by manuscript or other evidence will be reported.

The first modern attempt at a collected edition of Orlando di Lasso's music was the *Sämtliche Werke* (hereafter *SW*). Twenty-one volumes of this series appeared before the deteriorating financial climate in Germany forced its suspension in 1927. It published Lasso's settings of Italian, French, and German texts in its ten even-numbered volumes and 516 motets in its eleven odd-numbered volumes. Only after World War II was a continuation of *SW* undertaken, in the *Sämtliche Werke, neue Reihe* (hereafter *SWNR*), published by Bärenreiter in Kassel since 1956. This series is now essentially complete, and all of Lasso's music is finally available in print, but the editions vary greatly in quality. The motet volumes in *SW* were fundamentally flawed from the beginning, because their editor, Francis Xaver Haberl, chose as his primary source a posthumous compilation of Lasso's motets, rather than the authentic sources most closely associated with Lasso himself. This posthumous compilation, the *Magnum Opus Musicum* (*MOM*), was assembled by two of Lasso's sons, who printed his motets grouped according to the number of voice parts they contain, completely ignoring the chronology and the content of Lasso's original publications. Quite a few of the original editions, for instance, ordered the motets according to the eight modes which the individual pieces represented, an ordering that is completely obliterated in *SW*. Since the *SW* motet volumes are based on *MOM*, they do not facilitate the study of Lasso's development as a composer and the way in which he presented his music to the world. In addition, *MOM* in many instances contains faulty versions of text or music or both, which unfortunately have been perpetuated in the twentieth century by *SW*. They include arbitrary changes or omissions in the musical texts, incorrect placement of the words under the music, and in extreme cases replacement of the original words altogether (contrafacta). *SW* also retains the original clefs, which are a hindrance to many present-day performers and students.

Breitkopf und Härtel has begun to publish a revised edition of *SW,* under the editorial leadership of the Musikhistorische Kommission of the Bayerische

Akademie der Wissenschaften in Munich, which has also had charge of *SWNR*. Eight of the ten volumes of vernacular settings in *SW* have been issued in this revised edition (*SW2*), but work on the revision of the motet volumes has not even begun yet. When it will begin is unknown, and when it does, the revised volumes are not likely to appear in print for some years because of the hundreds of contemporary sources, mostly printed, that must be examined, evaluated, and collated. However, it appears that the unchronological format and the original clefs of the *MOM* and the old *SW* will be retained in the motet volumes of *SW2* as they have been in the vernacular works, with corrections of music or text made on copies of the *SW* pages. The result for the revised motet volumes of *SW* will be a reliable text in the old, chronologically jumbled order, with the original clefs retained. Given this situation, the need for a completely new edition of Lasso's motets is obvious, and this edition is intended to meet that need.

Volumes 1 and 23 of *SWNR* include eight motets that *MOM* and *SW* did not publish. They will be included in this edition for the sake of completeness, but other motet-like compositions (Officia, Lectiones, Lamentationes, Penitential Psalms, etc.) will be omitted, since they are already available in reliable editions. This edition will thus be limited almost entirely to the motets published in the old *SW*, with only two significant exceptions. First, the contents of the remarkable anthology known as the "Four-language print" of 1573 (*CM 10*; see table 1) are scattered among seven different volumes in *SW*. This collection deserves to be published at last as Lasso intended, with all the motets, lieder, chansons, and madrigals appearing together in their original ordering. Second, Ferdinand and Rudolph di Lasso published some of their own motets along with their father's work in 1597 and 1601; the sons' motets are not available in modern editions and will be included in *CM 20* as a supplement to Orlando's.

It is reasonable to ask how closely the chronology of the earliest sources of Lasso's motets corresponds to the chronology of their composition. A definitive answer is obviously impossible, but on the whole the correspondence seems to be very close. It appears that Lasso usually published his motets soon after their composition, so that the chronology of the original editions represents what we may reasonably assume to be their approximate order of composition (see table 1). To be sure, some of Lasso's works were printed only decades after their composition, notably the *Penitential Psalms* and the *Prophetiae sibyllarum*. The dates of these works and some masses and magnificats are established by manuscripts that predate publication by many years. Comparable situations among the motets, however, are almost nonexistent,

since the motets transmitted in *Hofkapelle* manuscripts were in most instances copied only a few years before or after their first editions. The most significant exceptions are fourteen *Hofkapelle* motets that were published only posthumously; they will appear in their appropriate chronological positions in *CM 17, 18,* and *19*. The present state of Lasso bibliography indicates that no first editions of the motets have been lost, so that the dates on which this edition is based are not likely to be revised in the future. In sum, the organization of this edition may be considered to represent the chronology both of the sources and of the composition of Lasso's motets, to the best of our present knowledge.

Each volume will include an introduction that discusses the music it contains and the sources of the music as well as texts and translations of any prefaces by Lasso himself; texts and translations; a few plates from the sources; the scores; the critical report, including (1) a description of the sources, (2) editorial methods, and (3) critical notes. An index for the entire edition is planned to appear in *CM 21*.

I wish to thank some individuals and institutions that have helped with the edition as a whole. Horst Leuchtmann of the Musikhistorische Kommission of the Bayerische Akademie der Wissenschaften allowed me free access to the Academy's rich storehouse of Lasso material, including his bibliography and sigla of Lasso prints and the Academy's microfilm collection. This has allowed me to put this edition on a firm bibliographic foundation and incorporate references to the forthcoming *Lasso-Verzeichnis* that will undoubtedly become the standard Lasso bibliography upon its publication. I am very grateful for Professor Leuchtmann's generosity and encouragement, which are well known to anyone who works in this field.

The Musikabteilung of the Bayerische Staatsbibliothek has the largest collection of Lasso sources in the world, and an edition such as this would be impossible without their assistance. Use of this library's materials will be acknowledged in many volumes of this edition, and I wish also to thank them here for their unfailing courtesy and efficiency, both when I have worked in Munich and when I have corresponded with them. I have of course consulted the previous editions of this music by Haberl, Sandberger, and Leuchtmann in *SW* and *SW2*, and I gladly acknowledge that they have made my own work and that of my collaborators much easier. Any flaws in this edition are not to be ascribed to them.

Major support for this edition has been provided by a grant from the National Endowment for the Humanities, an independent federal agency. Initial work on the edition was aided by a study grant from the Deutscher Akademischer Austauschdienst (DAAD). Funds for purchase of most of the microfilm used for

TABLE 1
Contents of the Edition

CM no.	Contents	RISM no.	LV no.	RRMR*
1	*Il primo libro di mottetti a cinque et a sei voci* (Antwerp, 1556) [17 motets for five and six voices]	1556a	1556-1	114
2	*Sacrae cantiones* (Nuremberg, 1562) [25 motets for five voices]	1562a	1562-4	
3	Motets for Four to Eight Voices from *Thesaurus musicus* (Nuremberg, 1564) [17 motets]	1564[1–5]	1564-5,6,7,8,9	
4	Motets for Six Voices from *Primus liber concentuum sacrorum* (Paris, 1564) [3 motets]	1564b	1564-5	105
	Motets for Four to Ten Voices from *Modulorum secundum volumen* (Paris, 1565) [21 motets]	1565a	1565-11	
5	Motets from *Quinque et sex voces perornatae sacrae cantiones* (Venice, 1565) [9 motets for five and six voices]	1565c	1565-4	109
	Sacrae cantiones, liber secundus, tertius, quartus (Venice, 1566) [17 motets for five to eight voices]	1566c,d,e	1566-7,8,9	
6	Motets for Four to Eight Voices from *Selectissimae cantiones* (Nuremberg, 1568) [20 motets]	1568a,b	1568-3,4	110
7	*Cantiones aliquot quinque vocum* (Munich, 1569) [14 motets for five voices]	1569a	1569-8	112
	Motets from *Selectiorum aliquot cantionum sacrarum sex vocum* (Munich, 1570) [10 motets for six voices]	1570c	1570-10	
8	*Moduli quinis vocis nunquam hactenus editi* (Paris, 1571) [19 motets for five voices]	1571a	1571-4	
9	*Patrocinium musices prima pars* (Munich, 1573) [21 motets for four, five, and six voices]	1573a	1573-9	
10	The Four-Language Print (Munich, 1573) [6 each of motets, chansons, madrigals, and lieder for four voices; 1 each for eight voices]	1573d	1573-8	102
11	*Liber mottettarum, trium vocum* (Munich, 1575) [18 motets for three voices]	1575b	1575-7	103
	Novae aliquot, ad duas voces cantiones (Munich, 1577) [24 motets for two voices]	1577c	1577-2	
12	*Sacrae cantiones quinque vocum* (Munich, 1582) [21 motets for five voices]	1582d	1582-6	
13	*Mottetta, sex vocum, typis nondum uspiam excusa* (Munich, 1582) [20 motets for six voices]	1582e	1582-7	
14	*Sacrae cantiones* (Munich, 1585) [31 motets for four voices; 1 for eight voices]	1585a	1585-8	111
15	*Cantica sacra sex et octo vocibus* (Munich, 1585) [15 motets for six voices; 1 motet for eight voices]	1585b	1585-4	
16	*Cantiones sacrae sex vocum* (Graz, 1594) [30 motets for six voices]	1594a	1594-2	
17	Motets from Printed Anthologies and Manuscripts, 1555–1569			115
18	Motets from Printed Anthologies and Manuscripts, 1570–1579			
19	Motets from Printed Anthologies and Manuscripts, 1580–1590			
20	*Cantiones quinque vocum* (Munich, 1597) [10 motets for five voices by Orlando di Lasso; 12 motets for five voices by Ferdinand di Lasso]	1597[3]	1597-1	
	Cantiones sacrae sex vocibus (Munich, 1601) [4 motets for six voices by Orlando di Lasso; 7 motets for six voices by Rudolph di Lasso]	1601[3]	1601-3	
21	Motets for Three to Twelve Voices from *Magnum Opus Musicum* (Munich, 1604) [61 motets transmitted only in *MOM*]	1604a	1604-1	

*RRMR gives the volume number as published in *Recent Researches in the Music of the Renaissance*. Those with no volume number listed are in progress.

the edition were made available through my Academic Support Account provided by the University of Oregon. Many colleagues have helped shape and refine plans for this edition during its gestation. I would particularly like to thank James Erb, University of Richmond; James Haar, University of North Carolina at Chapel Hill; Jessie Ann Owens, Brandeis University; David Crook, University of Wisconsin at Madison; Marian Smith and Anne Dhu McLucas of the School of Music, University of Oregon; the staff of the Office of Research and Sponsored Programs, University of Oregon; and the anonymous readers of the grant proposal submitted to the National Endowment for the Humanities. I should also like to thank the staff of A-R Editions for careful editing and production work that has greatly enhanced the appearance and clearness of this edition. My wife, Dorothy, has always been my strongest supporter and an active helper in my scholarly enterprises; without her involvement my work would be much more arduous. I thank these and other colleagues and friends too numerous to name for their contributions to this edition, which I hope will prove to be worthy of their support.

Peter Bergquist

Acknowledgments

Microfilm of the sources and permission to use them came from the following libraries: Musikabteilung der Bayerische Staatsbibliothek, Munich; Murhard'sche Bibliothek der Stadt und Landesbibliothek, Kassel; Civico Museo Bibliografico Musicale, Bologna; Bibliothèque Sainte-Geneviève, Paris; Bibliothèque Nationale, Paris; Österreichisches Nationalbibliothek, Vienna; British Library, London; Conservatorio di Musica Santa Cecilia, Rome; Bibliothèque Royale, Brussels; Biblioteka Gdańska Polskiej Akademii Nauk, Gdańsk. I am greatly indebted to my research assistant, Lorri Frogget, for her capable work on this and many other volumes of *CM*. I am most grateful for the assistance of Professor C. Bennett Pascal, University of Oregon, with the Latin texts and translations. Besides helping me be sure that the translations are accurate, he has many times suggested felicitous improvements in them, which I have been happy to adopt. The staff of Gerlach's Camera Centers, Eugene, has been extremely helpful and capable in preparing the plates for this and previous volumes of *CM*. Any faults that remain are my own responsibility.

Introduction

Volume 17 of Orlando di Lasso's *Complete Motets* contains twenty-six motets that were first published in printed collections or copied into manuscripts between 1555 and 1569. No more than six motets appear in any one printed source; the other pieces in each collection are variously settings of texts in vernacular languages, motets by composers other than Lasso, or motets by Lasso that had previously been published elsewhere. As a result, the contents of *CM 17* are much more varied than those of most other volumes in the series. The texts are almost equally divided between sacred and secular subjects, and the number of voices fluctuates between four and six. In the chronological ordering of this volume, the secular and sacred texts are mixed almost at random. Four of the secular motets were published as bowdlerized contrafacta in *MOM,* and *SW* published those versions of the texts rather than the originals. This volume prints the original texts; in some cases they appear for the first time in a modern edition.

The sources of *CM 17* are as varied as its contents, with a strong representation of the chanson and madrigal books in which many of the secular motets were published. Several of these sources survive incompletely, and the missing voice parts have to be found elsewhere; in a few instances only a single partbook is now extant, and the motets it contains are edited in whole or in part from later sources. The chronology of the motets according to their first editions has nonetheless been maintained, and the contents of *CM 17* appear in the order of their earliest printed sources with only one exception, "Dulces exuviae," Lasso's setting of Dido's farewell lament from Virgil's *Aeneid*. This exception points up the question of how closely the chronology of the sources corresponds to that of the composition of the motets, a question that is especially vexing in *CM 17*. "Dulces exuviae" was first published in 1570, but it was copied into a Munich manuscript some ten years earlier, and with such a considerable time difference it seemed proper to place the motet in *CM* according to the date of the manuscript rather than that of the

print. It is probable that other motets in this volume were composed some years before they were printed. In particular, some Italian prints probably contain pieces that Lasso composed in Italy before returning north in 1554, but no documentation supports this speculation.[1] It seems best to retain the ordering of the sources and provide comment about possible earlier dating in the discussions of the sources and the individual motets. In connection with these discussions the reader should consult the critical notes, where more details about the sources, including lists of contents, can be found.

The Sources

More than twenty printed and manuscript sources have been consulted in the preparation of *CM 17*. The earliest of the primary sources is one of Lasso's most famous and most thoroughly discussed publications, the collection of madrigals, villanesche, chansons, and motets for four voices published in Antwerp in 1555 by Tylman Susato in two issues, with titles respectively in French and Italian but with identical contents. These are *Le quatoirsiesme livre a quatre parties . . . faictz (a la Nouvelle composition d'aucuns d'Italie) par Rolando di Lassus* (RISM 1555a [1555[19]] = *LV* 1555-3) and *D'orlando di Lassus Il primo libro* (RISM 1555b [1555[29]] = *LV* 1555-2).[2] RISM 1555b was long believed to have been issued first, but Kristine Forney has established that RISM 1555a appeared first and underwent correction even before RISM 1555b was printed.[3] RISM 1555a/b are now popularly referred to as Lasso's "Opus 1," though his *Primo libro di madrigali a cinque voci,* published in Venice by Antonio Gardano in the same year (RISM 1555c = *LV* 1555-1) has an equal if not better claim to that designation. James Erb's introduction to *CM 1* makes this point, calling RISM 1555c a "proper 'Opus 1'," and goes on to observe that such a one-man publication, like a one-person show for an artist, signaled the composer's professional "arrival."[4] Such a debut for a twenty-three year old musician was remarkable, all the more so when one considers that the debut was simultaneous in Venice and Antwerp, with a different "show" in each city.

Forney's study has pointed out that soon after his arrival from Rome as an unknown composer, Lasso was somehow able to gain support for the publication of RISM 1555a/b from both Susato and Stefano Gentile, a prominent member of the Genoese "nation" or merchant colony in Antwerp, even though this caused an interruption in Susato's publishing program.[5] RISM 1555a contains no dedication, but Lasso dedicated RISM 1555b to Gentile, saying that it contains "a part of my efforts done in Antwerp at your request and under your protection after my return from Rome."[6] This can hardly mean that the entire contents of the collection were composed in Antwerp. The villanesche and most of the madrigals were very likely composed in Italy, the villanesche perhaps as early as 1551, when Lasso left Naples for Rome.[7] The motets are not so easy to date. Some may be of Roman origin, others composed shortly before publication, as is suggested below in the discussion of the individual motets.

The corrections to RISM 1555a, the *Quatuoirsiesme livre*, made in RISM 1555b, *Il primo libro*, had to do primarily with improving the underlay. Gathering E, which contains the motets, was one of the two parts of the book that was so corrected.[8] In fact, gathering E was entirely reset for the Italian issue,[9] which makes it especially unfortunate that that issue survives only as a superius partbook, while the French issue survives complete and has even been reprinted in facsimile. The underlay in the motets of RISM 1555a is indeed less than perfect, but the intended placement of the text is usually clear enough, even if some syllables are not positioned entirely accurately. The text of the motets in other respects is essentially error free, so the French issue provides a good basis for this edition, with no need to consult other sources for amendments.

The next earliest source represented in this volume is Munich, Bayerische Staatsbibliothek, Mus. Ms. 20, copied ca. 1560. Most of the manuscript is a nearly complete copy of Lasso's 1556 motet book published in Antwerp by Jan Laet, *Il primo libro de motetti a cinque et a sei voci* (RISM 1556a = *LV* 1556-1; see *CM 1*), but it includes three other motets as well: "Congratulamini mihi omnes" (*CM 6*), "Dulces exuviae," and "Pater, peccavi," nos. 7 and 14 in the present volume. Mus. Ms. 20 is an unreliable source with respect to text underlay, as noted in *CM 1* and *CM 5*, and its readings always have to be checked against other sources. Despite this deficiency, it predates the earliest printed source for "Dulces exuviae" by some ten years, so that motet is placed chronologically in this volume as composed ca. 1560. "Pater, peccavi" was

first published in 1564, so its manuscript source is close enough in time to the first edition that it has been placed according to the date of the printed source.

The *Tiers livre des chansons a quatre cincq et six parties* published in Louvain by Pierre Phalèse (RISM 1560b = *LV* 1560-4) contains, besides twenty-one chansons, many of them first editions, the two motets "Alma Venus" and "Tityre, tu patulae," nos. 8 and 9 in this volume. Its version of these motets is not fully satisfactory, especially in the text underlay, and in addition it includes only the first of the two parts of "Tityre, tu patulae," which must therefore be completed from a later source. Wolfgang Boetticher suggested that RISM 1560b might be a reprint of an earlier Susato edition now lost, since Susato was the "authorized" publisher of Lasso's chansons.[10]

In 1563 Antonio Barrè edited a collection of four-voice motets published in Venice by Francesco Rampazetto, *Liber primus musarum cum quattuor vocibus sacrarum cantionum* (RISM 1563[3] = *LV* 1563-3). Among its twenty-two motets are seven by Lasso, the five from RISM 1555a/b and two first editions, "Quia vidisti me, Thoma" and "Scio enim quod redemptor meus vivit," nos. 10 and 11 in this volume.

Pierre Phalèse's *Quatriesme livre des chansons a quatre et cincq parties* (RISM 1564d = *LV* 1564-3), published in Louvain, is the earliest known printed source for motets nos. 12–14 in this volume, "Fertur in conviviis," "Quid prodest stulto," and "Pater, peccavi." The first two of these are settings of texts congruent in subject and tone with the French texts in chanson books, but the inclusion in a chanson book of a full responsory text that comes from one of the gospels is decidedly unusual. As pointed out in the critical report, RISM 1564d's version of all three motets requires extensive emendation from other sources. Boetticher suggests that RISM 1564d, like 1560b, could be a reprint of a lost Susato book from a few years earlier, since Susato died in 1564.[11]

Le Roy and Ballard's *Dixhuictieme livre de chansons* (RISM 1565f = *LV* 1565-10) contains nine chansons for four and five voices, the six villanesche (here called "napolitaines") from RISM 1555a/b, and the chanson-motet "Deus qui bonum vinum creasti," no. 15 in this volume, for which it is the earliest known source. Its superius partbook does not survive, and that voice has been supplied from a later printing of the same book, RISM 1573i = *LV* 1573-17 (see the critical report).

Cipriano de Rore's posthumous *Quinto libro di madrigali a cinque voce* (RISM 1566[17] = *LV* 1566-13), published in Venice by Gardano, includes seven pieces by other composers, among them no. 16 in this volume, Lasso's secular motet "Forte soporifera." A motet book from the following year, *Primo libro de gli eterni mottetti di Orlando Lasso Cipriano Rore et d'altri eccel. musici* (RISM 1567[3] = *LV* 1567-13), published in Venice by Scotto, contains only one motet by Rore and four by Lasso. All four Lasso motets, nos. 17–20 in this volume, are first editions. Only the alto part-book survives, however, so for this volume these pieces have been edited from RISM 1568b (see the critical report).[12] Another Scotto print, *Secondo libro delle fiamme*, madrigals for five and six voices by various authors (RISM 1567[13] = *LV* 1567-10), includes Lasso's "S, U, su, P, E, R, per," no. 21 in this volume. The tenor partbook of RISM 1567[13] does not survive, and that voice has been supplied from a later reprint, RISM 1570[14] = *LV* 1570-11.

Antonio Gardano's series of five huge motet books entitled *Novus thesaurus* includes first editions of two Lasso motets in its first and third volumes (RISM 1568[2] = *LV* 1568-6 and RISM 1568[4] = *LV* 1568-8), "Audi, benigne conditor" and "Domine, quando veneris (2)," nos. 22 and 23 in this volume. Other Lasso motets it contains are reprints or simultaneous first editions with another publisher.

The final primary source for this volume is *Liber secundus sacrarum cantionum quatuor vocum . . . auctoribus Orlando di Lassus. Cypriano de Rore.*, published in Louvain by Phalèse (RISM 1569[8] = *LV* 1569-11). Among its nine Lasso motets are three first editions, "Tribulationem et dolorem inveni," "Laetentur caeli," and "Fratres, sobrii estote," nos. 24–26 in this volume. Unlike other Phalèse motet sources used in this volume, its text is quite accurate.

The Music and Texts

"Audi dulcis amica mea": The four motets in RISM 1555a/b that set sacred texts may well have been composed a few years earlier, in Italy before Lasso's return north. No external or internal evidence provides a firm date for any one of them. The style is surely early; "Audi dulcis amica mea" in particular, with its extensive text repetitions, does not reflect Lasso's usual economy of utterance. The passage in coloration at "Nigra es sed formosa" is a madrigalian commonplace of the time, as Boetticher remarks,[13] but perhaps it also is an early indication of Lasso's inclination to respond to the text. On the other hand, the striking octave descent made by the outer voices in parallel tenths in measures 31–35 does not seem to be text related. It is noteworthy that all four sacred motets in RISM 1555a/b are on texts that other composers had previously set, which is true of few other motets in this volume. The previous setting of "Audi dulcis amica mea" by Jacquet of Mantua is especially interesting in this regard because it is one of the few instances in the Lasso motets where it is at all possible to suggest imitation or emulation by Lasso.[14] His

melodic motives for the words "Audi dulcis amica mea" (altus and bassus), "Nigra es sed formosa," "ideo amore tuo," and "et quia tribulor" bear more than a casual resemblance to Jacquet's settings of the same words. The resemblances do not go beyond the first several notes, and Jacquet does not use coloration at "Nigra es," but the similarities seem somewhat more than coincidental. They could point toward an Italian origin for this motet, since Jacquet was active mainly in Mantua, where he "dominated musical life" from 1534 to 1559.[15]

"Peccantem me quotidie": Earlier settings of this responsory from the Office for the Dead were made by Crecquillon, Clemens, Mouton, Jacquet de Berchem, and Morales, none of which shows any resemblance to Lasso's. Most of these set the full respond with repetendum plus verse with repetendum.[16] As is often the case, Lasso set only the respond portion. His motet begins with step-wise motion within a narrow compass, which prepares the dramatic contrast of octave leaps at the words "et non me paenitentem." At "Miserere mei, Deus" Lasso repeats the traditional semitone motive favored by so many composers beginning with Josquin.

"Inclina Domine aurem tuam": Psalm 85 was set complete or in part before Lasso's motet by Sermisy, Clemens, Gombert, Jacotin, and Conrad Rein. None of these motets includes exactly the same verses as Lasso's, and none of them have any musical resemblance to Lasso's. Boetticher perhaps carries his apparent fondness for finding suggestions of villanella style in the motets too far when he makes that observation about the setting of "quoniam inops et pauper sum" in this motet.[17] However, he observes with good reason that Lasso's inclination to divide a four-voice texture into voice pairs is already found in the earliest works and derives from Josquin and Clemens.[18]

"Domine, quando veneris (1)": Here again Lasso set only the respond portion of a responsory, unlike Clemens, who set the complete text in two parts.[19] A striking bit of text illustration occurs at the words "ubi me abscondam" when the voices move in turn with very active melismas, followed by complete silence at the beginning of measure 32. Boetticher notes that this device is not found in Clemens's setting.[20]

"Alma Nemes": This motet more than any other piece in RISM 1555a is "composed in the new manner of some Italians," as the title page proclaims. Donna Cardamone suggests that it may have been composed in Antwerp at the request of Stefano Gentile

> to honor a female singer known as Nemes. The final lines not only pay tribute to her extraordinary vocal powers, but they allude to personal engagement with the composer himself, a capable singer . . . Nemes was

probably a woman of high birth from Gentile's inner circle. Her pseudo-antique name referring to Nemesis—the nymph goddess of due enactment—is reminiscent of an academic tradition in which members took nicknames that stress, by ironical paradox, some personal quality. In Lasso's expressive construction of Nemes, she is endowed with the positive attributes of a divine enchantress and figuratively entrusted with the responsibility of transmitting music "composed in the new manner of some Italians."[21]

Ignace Bossuyt adds an interesting suggestion about the identity of the poet. He discovered that the poem of the opening piece in RISM 1555a/b, the sestina "Del freddo Rheno," was published with a number of other poems that formed a supplement to Stefano Ambrosio Schiappalaria's translation into ottava rima of Virgil's *Aeneid*, book 4. Plantin published the book in Antwerp in 1568; some of the poems were as much as twenty years old.[22] In "Del freddo Rheno" the narrator encounters a beautiful young woman with a charming voice, whom in the fifth stanza he addresses as "Oh Neme." Bossuyt suggests that appearance of this unusual name links "Del freddo Rheno" with "Alma Nemes" and that the same author wrote both poems. Schiappalaria resided in Antwerp for a long time, and it appears likely that he and Gentile provided Lasso with these texts in honor of a singer within their circle.

The chromatic style of "Alma Nemes" is comparable to that of Lasso's *Prophetiae sibyllarum,* which most probably date from two or three years later, soon after Lasso's arrival in Munich.[23] Edward Lowinsky among others has called special attention to the chord succession in "Alma Nemes" that sets the words "dulce novumque melos," moving from an F♯ major triad in measure 51 through major triads on B, E, A, and D to G major in measure 54.[24] It is indeed wideranging, exceeding on both the sharp and flat sides what David Crook has termed Lasso's "normative tonal compass," extending from the pitch A♯ in measure 51 to E♭ in measure 26.[25] Apt as this illustration is, one might note that the chromaticism in the rest of the motet is not so specifically text-related. In *MOM* "Alma Nemes" appeared with a substitute text that begins "Alme Deus" and was consequently published in *SW* in that form. The contrafactum does not appear in any publication during Lasso's lifetime.[26]

"Calami sonum ferentes": This famous motet by Cipriano de Rore was first published in RISM 1555a/b. It is so obviously a companion to "Alma Nemes" that its inclusion in this volume of *CM* seems appropriate, although it recently has been published elsewhere. Lowinsky has provided what may be the last word on this motet in his extended study first published in 1989.[27] He discovered the author of the

poem, Giovanni Battista Pigna (1530–75), and consulted with Arthur W. H. Adkins, who found that each line of the poem uses a different meter drawn from isolated lines in the poems of Catullus. Lowinsky also proposed that because of the "rough harmonic texture, with extreme chromaticism, in the muddled sound of four basses" Rore intended the motet as an anti-chromatic manifesto against the innovations of Nicola Vicentino.[28] Rore was no stranger to chromaticism in other works, of course, but "Calami sonum ferentes" is exceedingly ungainly compared to any of Rore's other works that explore a chromatic style.

In the present context, Lasso's connection with Rore's motet is of greatest interest. Here too Lowinsky has a convincing theory. He rejects Boetticher's suggestion that Susato was responsible for including "Calami sonum ferentes" in RISM 1555a/b,[29] postulating instead a visit by Lasso to Ferrara in 1553 to 1554, while he was maestro da capella at St. John Lateran in Rome.[30] On that occasion Rore and Lasso presumably met, and Rore, impressed by the young man, allowed him to copy the motet, which he had no intention of publishing (it was in fact published in Venice in 1561, but probably without Rore's participation). Lasso then gave Rore's motet the place of honor at the end of his new publication and included his own chromatic essay with it as a tribute to Rore, though steering clear of the bizarre qualities of Rore's manifesto. Bossuyt proposes an alternate scenario, that Gentile could have provided Rore's motet to Lasso, since the connections between Italy and Antwerp were after all musical as well as commercial.[31] In either case, it seems that Rore's motet should appear in *CM 17* following Lasso's, just as it did in RISM 1555a/b.

"Dulces exuviae": This motet and the two that follow it form a distinct group within *CM 17.* All three set classical or classicistic texts in a declamatory style that is more often homophonic than imitative, a style to which Lasso occasionally returned in later years.[32] Helmuth Osthoff's study of sixteenth-century settings of passages from the *Aeneid* discusses the many settings of Dido's farewell prior to Lasso's.[33] They have in common a tendency to favor expression of the text over faithfulness to poetic meter. Lasso's setting, which uses more lines of the *Aeneid* than any other, is most closely related to Willaert's, with which it shares a declamatory style, in contrast to their more strongly linear predecessors.[34] Osthoff notes the "monumental-pathetic" character of Lasso's setting and its indirect chromaticism, which however does not exceed the normative tonal compass for its tonal type. As noted above, the earliest source for this motet is Munich, Bayerische Staatsbibliothek, Mus. Ms. 20, which was copied about ten years before the earliest printed source, *Mellange d'Orlande de Lassus* (Paris: Le Roy and Ballard, RISM 1570d = *LV* 1570-6). Both sources have been consulted for the present edition.

"Alma Venus": The earliest source for this motet and "Tityre, tu patulae" is Pierre Phalèse's *Tiers livre des chansons a quatre cincq et six parties* (RISM 1560b). A contrafactum of "Alma Venus" was published in Nuremberg in Gerlach's *Selectissimae cantiones* (RISM 1568b) under the title "Christe, Patris verbum," and both versions circulated during Lasso's lifetime.[35] The original version was published only in chanson books, in Phalèse's *Tiers livre* and its reprints, in Le Roy and Ballard's *Quinsieme livre de chansons* (RISM 1564[11] = *LV* 1564-12 and RISM 1565[7] = *LV* 1565-13), and their *Mellange* (RISM 1570d with expanded reprints in 1576 and 1586).[36] The somewhat faulty text of "Alma Venus" in RISM 1560b has been emended from Le Roy and Ballard's *Meslanges* (RISM 1576i = *LV* 1576-7) as a representative of that strand of transmission. The motet sets a neo-Latin poem in self-proclaimed elegiacs in the declamatory style Lasso used for classical texts. Boetticher associates the poem's subject with that of "Alma Nemes," which seems true only to the extent that both mention the powers of music.[37] "Alma Venus" invokes good fortune and celebrates its achievement, while "Alma Nemes" lauds the powers of an accomplished singer. To speak of both motets in the same breath as chromatic pieces also seems strained, since "Alma Venus" does not exceed Lasso's normative compass.[38]

"Tityre, tu patulae": This motet has a complex publishing history. Its first part was printed in Phalèse's *Tiers livre des chansons* (RISM 1560b), but its second *pars* did not appear until RISM 1568a, Gerlach's *Selectissimae cantiones*. I stated incorrectly in *CM 6* that the second part was first published in Le Roy and Ballard's *Quatorsiesme livre de chansons* (RISM 1564[10] = *LV* 1564-10),[39] but that book and its earlier edition (RISM 1561[6] = *LV* 1561-3) contain only the first part. Reprints of the *Tiers livre* through 1573 continued to include only the first part, but Le Roy and Ballard printed both parts in their *Mellange*, RISM 1570d, and in its successors. The first part in RISM 1560b contains many errors in both music and text underlay, and the Le Roy and Ballard *Quatorsiesme livre* is much more accurate. RISM 1568a corrects most of the errors in the first part of the motet, in which it is essentially identical to RISM 1570d and 1576i. The second part in RISM 1568a is largely free of errors and is nearly identical to RISM 1576i, which has been used to represent the French strand of transmission of the motet. A few corrections in both parts have been supplied from RISM 1579a, Leonhard Lechner's expanded reissue of RISM 1568a.

A reliable text for both parts of "Tityre, tu patulae" can thus be established from the later editions of the piece. The delayed publication of the second part demands explanation: was the delay caused by inadvertence or accident, or was the second part composed only some years after the first? The absence of the second part in the first eight years of the motet's publication history suggests strongly that the second part did not exist or was not known to either Phalèse or Le Roy and Ballard. However, other evidence about "Tityre, tu patulae" is available. On 23 December 1559 Dr. Georg Sigmund Seld, the Bavarian vice-chancellor and legate, wrote Duke Albrecht V from Vienna, recounting that on the previous day he had heard a polyphonic mass sung in the imperial chapel:

> The theme upon which it was written seemed familiar to my ears but I could not recognize it immediately. Later, as I sang it over, I realized that the royal *Kapellmeister* had composed it on the model of the *Tityre, tu patulae* by Orlando. As I know that Your Highness does not possess this [mass] I shall take care to send it to you. I truly believe that it will not at all displease you.[40]

The unnamed kapellmeister was Jacob Vaet. A later undated letter states:

> Your Majesty ought to know that the royal *Kapellmeister* composed a six-voice motet, namely, *Vitam quam faciunt beatiorum* in which he desired to imitate [the style of] Orlando's *Tityre, tu patulae*. The mass is based on both motets. I am therefore sending to Your Highness the said *Vitam quam faciunt* as well.[41]

Seld's letter shows that at the end of 1559 Lasso's motet had been in existence long enough for Jacob Vaet to have composed a mass and motet in imitation of it. Vaet's motet (the correct title is "Vitam quae faciunt beatiorum") was published in 1558 in Nuremberg by Berg and Neuber in the first book of their *Novum et insigne opus musicum* (RISM 1558[4]), which pushes the date of Lasso's motet back even earlier, very close to the beginning of his service at the Bavarian court. It could even be possible that Lasso composed the piece prior to his arrival in Munich. This would be consistent with Boetticher's suggestion that RISM 1560b may have been preceded by a Susato edition now lost, since Phalèse was not usually an authorized publisher of Lasso's chansons.[42]

A comparison of Vaet's motet and masses with "Tityre, tu patulae" yields additional conclusions. To begin with, Dr. Seld seems to be literally correct when he says that Vaet imitated the style of Lasso's motet, in the sense that he followed its style (as Steinhardt's interpolation in the second letter suggests) rather than borrowing its substance. I find no musical material whatsoever from Lasso's motet in Vaet's motet, with the possible exception of a few chord progressions set to a different rhythm.[43] Consequently Vaet's *Missa Vitam quae faciunt beatiorem* contains nothing of Lasso beyond its general style, which is shared among all four compositions under consideration. I cannot find a clear reference to Lasso's motet in this mass. On the other hand, Vaet's *Missa Tityre, tu patulae* is obviously an imitation or parody mass, with frequent references in the mass to its model, *but only to its first part.* The mass behaves in every respect like a parody mass based on the first part of "Tityre, tu patulae," with a clear, almost literal reference to the beginning of the motet at beginnings of the Kyrie, Gloria, and Agnus Dei, and with a more manipulated reference at the beginning of the Credo. The endings of each movement of the mass refer to the last measures of the first part of the motet more or less directly, and other references to interior segments of the motet's first part may be found during the course of the movements of the mass. The mass also refers several times to Vaet's own motet, as Dr. Seld said.

The first part of "Tityre, tu patulae," then, was quite likely composed near the time that Lasso came to Munich. It became known in Vienna soon afterwards and was parodied in a mass by Jacob Vaet, and its style was emulated in Vaet's motet, "Vitam quae faciunt beatiorem." It was first published in 1560, as far as we now know, and was reprinted several times before its second part appeared in print in 1568. We have no basis for dating the second part any earlier, and it appears likely that Lasso composed the second part some years after the first part, perhaps as many as ten years. The precise time difference is uncertain because of the possibility that the second part existed in manuscript before 1568, but it seems safe to assert that the second part did not yet exist when Vaet composed his mass based on the first part, nor did it yet exist when the first part was originally published.

As remarked above, "Tityre, tu patulae" uses the declamatory style that Lasso favored for several classical or classicistic poems. This style is followed in Vaet's motet, which Boetticher associates with Lasso's as an expression of the "musica reservata" ideal.[44] Dr. Seld is also invoked as one who used the term "reservata." One might argue that a direct, uncomplicated approach to the text such as is found in this motet is contrary to many understandings of the term "reservata," which stress more elaborate artifice of one sort or another.[45] Pieces like this seem to have been very popular, in any case, given the sixteen known printings of "Tityre, tu patulae" through 1619, the year of the final issue of the *Meslanges* (RISM 1619b = *LV* 1619-2). Seven printings included only the first part, which ends on the same final as the second part and is thus self-contained tonally. The first part is also complete textually, since it includes Meliboeus's invo-

cation to Tityrus, while the second part sets Tityrus's response. Could Duke Albrecht have suggested to Lasso, once he had heard the first part, that the motet be enlarged to encompass Tityrus's contribution to the dialogue?

"Quia vidisti me, Thoma" and "Scio enim quod redemptor meus vivit": These two motets were first published in Venice by Rampazetto in the *Liber primus musarum cum quattuor vocibus* (RISM 1563[3]) edited by Antonio Barrè. Lasso is the composer most strongly represented in this anthology, which contains among its twenty-two motets the five from RISM 1555a/b plus the two new ones. Boetticher suggests that Barrè obtained these motets from Roman sources and that Lasso had thus composed them there about ten years before they were published.[46] This is plausible for the two first editions, since Barrè also published Lasso madrigals that he said he gathered from copies found in Italy (see note 1 above), but one need not assume that the other five motets were obtained in this same way rather than copied from RISM 1555a/b or one of its reissues. "Alma Nemes" was fairly certainly composed in Antwerp (see the discussion of that motet above), and possibly others of the five were as well. Barrè describes the motets of RISM 1563[3] as printed for the first time, but Boetticher rightly observes that this probably means printed for the first time in Italy.[47] Boetticher failed to observe that "Scio enim quod redemptor meus vivit" is included in RISM 1563[3], since he lists Gerlach's *Selectissimae cantiones* (RISM 1568b) as its earliest source.[48]

These two motets are stylistically similar to those of RISM 1555a/b, and they are probably among Lasso's earliest surviving motets. Noel O'Regan calls attention to a musical exchange between Munich and Rome in 1562 which conceivably could have included the two motets first printed in Barrè's anthology, but he suggests that Lasso probably would have sent something more up-to-date, since all the motets in RISM 1563[3] are "stylistically similar, examples of standard mid-century Franco-Flemish imitative polyphony, characterized in particular by long melismatic lines."[49] This is an apt description of both "Quia vidisti me, Thoma" and "Scio enim quod redemptor meus vivit," though each has features that point to Lasso as its composer. In "Quia vidisti me, Thoma" the repetitions of "et crediderunt" from measure 32 on, frequently as a descending fifth, build effectively to the cadence in measures 44–45. In the following "alleluia" the bassus repeats the same motive sequentially eleven times, while the upper voices are constantly varied. The text of "Scio enim quod redemptor meus vivit" is the respond from Responsory 1 in Matins of the Office for the Dead, and this text is also included in *Lectio* 8 for the same service. Lasso set the same text as part of the *lectio* a few years later in his *Lectiones ex Propheta Iob,* and a comparison between the two settings is instructive.[50] The motet passes over the opportunity to illustrate the words "in novissimo die," which in the *Lectiones* are the occasion for an excursion to an F♯ minor triad. Both pieces respond to "surrecturus sum," the motet with an ascending line that is followed by a rest on a strong beat, the *lectio* with the leap of an octave. The motet repeats "videbo Deum" homorhythmically three times, the third with the same C–B♭–C chord progression Lasso uses for the single statement of those words in the *lectio*. The *Lectiones* in general are more adventurous in responding to their texts, which strengthens the assumption that the motet is an earlier work.

"Fertur in conviviis": This and the two following motets in this volume were first published in Louvain in Phalèse's *Quatriesme livre des chansons a quatre et cincq parties* (RISM 1564d). Bernhold Schmid's study of this piece has thoroughly illuminated its checkered publishing history, in which so many variants and contrafacta of its text are found in the twenty-two known printed sources between 1564 and 1604.[51] Most of these sources are chanson books, and both in its style and the content of its text "Fertur in conviviis," a motet in name only, is closely related to the chanson. Schmid's exploration of the origins of its text traces it back to portions of a poem by the Archpoet, the "Confession of Golias" that is included in the *Carmina burana* as no. 191. Through the three centuries of its transmission this poem underwent considerable variation in its contents and their ordering. The text Lasso set is in effect part of this unstable tradition that continued through the sixteenth century and beyond. Many of Lasso's Latin drinking songs were published in *MOM* and *SW* as contrafacta; in "Fertur in conviviis" those editions turned the sense around completely, from a song in praise of wine to a song condemning it. The parodistic inclusion of the chant incipit "Requiem aeternam" at the end of the motet would have been especially offensive to Counter-Reformation sensibilities, but since it could not be omitted, the rest of the text was changed so that it was no longer humorous. Although the texts of all three motets in RISM 1564d are faulty and require emendation from other sources, the poem of "Fertur in conviviis" is error free. I have chosen therefore to reproduce its text from RISM 1564d rather than incorporate the small variants that appear in the numerous reprints by Le Roy and Ballard, which Schmid presents as the basic text of the poem. Even though Le Roy and Ballard's version was distributed more widely, I believe lines 2–3 have more pungency when they read "masculinum displicet atque foemininum,

| sed in neutro genere vinum est divinum" rather than ". . . placet femininum; | et in neutro genere. . . ."

. "Quid prodest stulto": The critical report for this motet shows in detail the inaccuracy of the text presented in RISM 1564d, which is my reason for using Gardano's error-free printing in *Sacrae cantiones liber secundus* (RISM 1566c = *LV* 1566-7) as the primary source. Gardano presents a lightly edited version of the first Italian printing of this motet in Scotto's *Quinque et sex vocibus perornatae sacrae cantiones* (RISM 1565c = *LV* 1565-4); the differences between Phalèse and the Italian sources are such that they appear to represent two distinct textual traditions. Gardano's version was followed in most of the twenty-two printings of this motet through 1619, nine of which were issued in chanson books by Le Roy and Ballard in Paris, beginning with their *Dixsetieme livre de chansons* (RISM 1565[9] = *LV* 1565-9). The sources also include six motet books, and the moralistic, though not specifically religious, biblical text probably allowed the motet to fit comfortably into either a sacred or secular collection. The music itself probably contributes to this duality as well. James Haar describes the cantus firmus in tenor 1 as "set to an odd, quasi-palindromic melody, in semiminims and minims, of an almost flippant character, about as far removed from the cantus firmus norm as possible."[52] The other voices move more sedately when the motet begins, but they gradually take on more of the animation of the cantus firmus, and when the latter reaches and holds its last note the other voices conclude with both the text and rhythm of the cantus firmus.

"Pater, peccavi": The first edition of this motet in RISM 1564d followed by some four years its entry into Mus. Ms. 20. As stated in the critical report, I have corrected these two sources when necessary from RISM 1565a and 1568b, in which the text underlay is improved. In this motet Lasso set the complete text of a responsory, both respond and verse, in contrast to his more frequent settings of a respond only. Several earlier composers set the complete responsory, including Clemens, Willaert, Crecquillon, and Jean Conseil.[53] Lasso's setting has nothing in common with any of these. Its opening measures have a slight resemblance to the *exordium* of Rore's "Quanti mercenarii," but because Rore set only the verse of the responsory, the texts of the two *exordia* are not the same.[54] A more interesting relationship exists between Lasso's motet and a setting of the same text by Andrea Gabrieli, first published in his *Sacrae cantiones liber primus* by Gardano in Venice in 1565 (RISM G 49). Marie Louise Göllner has observed that Gabrieli was quite likely in residence at the Bavarian court around 1565 through 1566,[55] so he would have been able to hear and probably perform Lasso's motet and model his own on it. The relationship is closest in tonal type (low clefs, one flat, final F) and the five-voice setting with two cantus parts, which both motets have in common. However, Gabrieli seems not to quote Lasso's motet even indirectly, despite the opportunities offered by the common structural elements.

"Deus qui bonum vinum creasti": This secular motet was first printed by Le Roy and Ballard in their *Dixhuictieme livre de chansons* (RISM 1565f, reprinted RISM 1573i), and thereafter in their *Mellange* (RISM 1570d) and its reissues. The original text was retained by Simon Goulart in his *Thrésor de Musique d'Orlande de Lassus* (Geneva, RISM 1576l [1576⁴] = LV 1576-5) and its reprints, in which so many of the French texts were "purified."[56] A contrafactum published only in *MOM* and in *SW* totally misrepresents the spirited wit of the original text and the music to which Lasso set it. The original text is a parody of a collect or prayer, in which a drinker asks for the good sense at least for the company to find their beds. The typical structure of a collect is followed, beginning with an invocation to God and acknowledgment of His power ("Deus qui bonum vinum creasti et ex eodem multa capita dolere fecisti"). Then follows a petition ("da nobis quaesumus intellectum") and the intention or benefit requested ("ut saltem possimus invenire lectum.") This structure may be found in almost any collect or prayer in the Editio Vaticana and in many vernacular prayer books.[57] Lasso stresses the word "dolere" with drawn out semitone figures, then the bassus almost literally sinks into bed from measure 35 on. Small wonder that the piece was published only in chanson books, since it belongs more to this genre than to that of the motet.

"Forte soporifera": This motet was first published in Cipriano de Rore's *Quinto libro di madrigali a cinque voci* by Antonio Gardano (RISM 1566¹⁷). It was not circulated too widely thereafter, appearing only in Gerlach's *Selectissimae cantiones* (RISM 1568b) and its reprints and in Le Roy and Ballard's *Mellange* (RISM 1570d), though it was dropped from their 1576 and 1586 reissues. In *MOM* and *SW* its text was somewhat altered to tone down the eroticism. Perhaps the latter is not the main point of the poem, however. C. Bennett Pascal suggests that it is an etiological myth for the origin of a hot spring; in a similar myth the springs at Abano were attributed to furrows plowed by Hercules with the oxen of Geryon.[58] If this is the intention of "Forte soporifera," it could be difficult to establish which hot springs may be referred to. Gardano's dedication of RISM 1566¹⁷ to Ottavio Farnese, Duke of Parma and Piacenza, perhaps suggests the area in which to look.[59]

"Quis est homo qui timet Dominum?": This is one of the four motets in this volume that first appeared in *Primo libro de gli eterni mottetti di Orlando Lasso Cipriano Rore et d'altri eccel. mvsici* (RISM 1567³), edited by Giulio Bonagiunta and published in Venice by Scotto. Since only the alto part book of this source survives, these motets have been edited from the next earliest source that survives complete, Gerlach's *Selectissimae cantiones* (RISM 1568a and b). Giulio Ongaro suggests plausibly that Bonagiunta may have received these four motets directly from Lasso when he visited Venice in 1567. Lasso's main business on that visit was overseeing the production of his fourth book of madrigals, so he might well have given or sold to Bonagiunta a few new motets that he himself did not have time to bring out.[60] Bonagiunta had edited motets by Lasso two years earlier, according to his own statement with Lasso's permission,[61] so Lasso may well have had dealings with him again in 1567. Presumably Gerlach obtained the motets from Lasso or from Scotto's edition and published them in Nuremberg a year later. "Quis est homo qui timet Dominum?" sets two verses of Psalm 24 that appear to have no specified liturgical use as a unit. They may have been set simply because of their optimistic content, according to Boetticher, who notes that after 1560 Lasso increasingly turned to psalm texts that emphasize goodness and mercy.[62]

"Ubi est Abel": This motet text is yet another instance in which Lasso set only the respond section of a responsory. Boetticher finds that the opening phrase is combined with the middle section ("Nescio, Domine") in the close ("Ecce vox sanguinis") in "downright atomistic motivic work" (geradezu atomarer Motivverarbeitung).[63] Motivic resemblances among those sections perhaps exist, especially the descending thirds; it is not clear what he means by "atomistic." The motet is an excellent setting of an affective text; the descent to "terra" at the end is especially noteworthy.

"Quem dicunt homines": This motet divides the text of the respond from a responsory into two parts. Three earlier settings of the same text by Richafort, Pionnier, and Gombert are conveniently accessible in a volume of *Das Chorwerk* edited by Lewis Lockwood.[64] All three of them set the complete text of the responsory except for the words "dixit Jesus discipulis suis." Boetticher mentions this motet in connection with other Gospel settings that he suggests Lasso composed in the 1560s, though the earliest sources of some are dated as late as 1582. He connects these motets to Lasso's especially close relationships with Protestant audiences at the time, and suggests that both the quantity of Gospel settings and the Protestant connections declined after 1570.[65] One may reasonably hesitate to make a causal connection between the two circumstances. Gospel settings were, as Boetticher notes, especially favored in Protestant regions of Germany, and Lasso's connections with them may have been especially close before 1570, but his popularity and influence certainly continued strongly in northern Germany well after his own death. "Quem dicunt homines" in any case may not be the best example in such a discussion, since its text is one of the foundations of the Roman Catholic claim to primacy, though Protestants would of course interpret it differently.

"Jesu, nostra redemptio": This six-voice hymn-motet in four parts forms a group with "Jesu, corona virginum" and "Vexilla regis prodeunt" from *CM 5* and "Veni Creator Spiritus" from *CM 6*. All four are scored for the same combination that includes two altus and two bassus voice parts, and except for "Veni Creator Spiritus," the third part of each is a duo. "Audi, benigne conditor," no. 22 in this volume, is closely related to them but is on a smaller scale, with only two parts and five voices, two of them nonetheless bassi. In a study of parody masses by Ivo de Vento and Andrea Gabrieli based respectively on "Jesu, nostra redemptio" and "Vexilla regis prodeunt," Marie Louise Göllner has noted the rich texture of these motets, the florid writing for the bass voices especially, and the frequent text illustration.[66] Since Vento's parody mass is dated "1565" in its manuscript source,[67] Lasso's motet is to be dated three or more years earlier than its first publication.

"S, U, su, P, E, R, per": This is without a doubt one of the silliest pieces ever committed to paper by a major composer. Lasso was of course no stranger to using serious texts in the most incongruistically parodistic contexts, but this piece goes far beyond the occasional chant quotations found in drinking songs, such as "Fertur in conviviis." The first verse of Psalm 136, a lament of the exiled Jews in Babylon, is shredded into its component letters and syllables and reassembled piece by piece, in a process that recalls nursery songs or the organized cheers at athletic events. The text is neither onomatopoeic or stuttering, rather a systematic deconstruction of a serious psalm verse. The parody is only in the text; the music resembles in style a villanella or chanson more than a motet. It was first published in a madrigal book, *Secondo libro delle fiamme*, issued in Venice by Girolamo Scotto (RISM 1567[13]), in which the other fifteen pieces appear to have typical Italian madrigal texts. It was published the next year by Gerlach in his large motet collection *Selectissimae cantiones* (RISM 1568b) and retained in the later editions, and Le Roy and Ballard included it in their anthology of Lasso's chansons, the *Mellange* (1570d) and its expanded reprints through 1619. The field thus seems completely open for a designation of the piece's genre. Such play with words

immediately brings to mind Lasso's own linguistic foolery in so many of his letters to the future Duke Wilhelm V.[68] Boetticher suggests the frottola, the commedia dell'arte, the moresca, and the chanson as possible sources for the nonsense syllables, also a possible allusion to the confused speech at the tower of Babel.[69] The latter is out of context for the exiles in Babylon, and while the various musical sources may have contributed to Lasso's inspiration, I am more inclined to credit his own inventive sense of humor. In performance the letters and syllables should most probably be sounded as present-day Germans pronounce Latin, which is likely to be close to what Lasso's own musicians would have done.

"Audi, benigne conditor": As mentioned above, this hymn-motet is on a smaller scale than its companions from the same time period. It shares nonetheless their inclination towards expression of textual details (such as the $\frac{6}{3}$ chords in a chain of suspensions at "poenasque comparavimus," mm. 68–75), and the two bassus voices are notably florid in this piece as in the other hymn-motets. This motet was not reprinted during Lasso's lifetime. After its first edition in Gardano's *Novi thesauri musici liber primus* (RISM 1568[2]), edited by Petrus Joanellus, it next appeared only in *MOM*.

"Domine, quando veneris (2)": This five-voice setting of the same text used in no. 4 of this volume also was first published by Gardano, in *Novi atque catholici thesauri musici liber tertius* (RISM 1568[4]). Lasso's sons either did not know of this motet or chose to omit it when they assembled *MOM*. As a result, it was not published in *SW*, and its first modern edition was that of Boetticher in the revised first volume (1989) of *SWNR*.[70] Boetticher suggests that the sons confused this motet with the earlier four-voice version, not realizing that they are two different compositions. He remarks that even though this motet was published in an anthology, there is no doubt of its authenticity, and that it is a beautiful piece with a thicker texture than the earlier setting.[71] The motet is indeed more polyphonic and less declamatory than Lasso's norm, but I would agree that it is surely authentic. I found the ascriptions of two other motets first published by Gardano and omitted from *MOM* and *SW* highly questionable,[72] but "Domine, quando veneris (2)" is entirely worthy of Lasso. Perhaps Joanellus or Gardano obtained it and "Audi, benigne conditor" from the composer during his visit to Venice in 1567.

"Tribulationem et dolorem inveni," "Laetentur caeli," and "Fratres, sobrii estote": The last three motets in this volume were first published by Phalèse in Louvain in *Liber secundus sacrarum cantionum quatuor vocum* (RISM 1569[0]), a collection of nine motets by Lasso and five by Rore. Besides the three first editions, the Lasso motets include pieces from RISM 1555b, 1563[3], 1564d, and one movement from the *Lectiones* from Job. All three were reprinted later by Le Roy and Ballard and by Gerlach. Boetticher in fact was unaware that "Tribulationem et dolorem inveni" was included in RISM 1569[8], since he stated that Le Roy and Ballard's *Moduli quatuor et octo vocum* (RISM 1572b = *LV* 1572-7) is its earliest known edition.[73]

All three motets show Lasso in his finest four-voice vein. "Tribulationem et dolorem inveni" is the darkest text of the three, and the psalmist's plea for God's help, measures 27–36, is especially impressive with its octave leaps in the bassus. "Laetentur caeli" has a joyful text that stimulated Lasso to frequent exuberant melismas. The rhetoric of "Fratres, sobrii estote" is striking throughout, beginning with the opening admonition that is set off by a fermata. "Sobrii" and "vigilate" are neatly contrasted through varied rhythmic pace, then the "adversarius" is characterized by parallel $\frac{6}{3}$ chords, a device Lasso sometimes associates with sin or weakness. The roaring lion literally circles about ("circuit"), and finally the brothers are urged to resist ("resistite") in strenuous cross-rhythms that finally close firmly and solidly ("fortes in fide").

Notes

1. This is in contrast to the early madrigal books, in which the prefaces strongly suggest that they are collections of pieces Lasso wrote in Italy but did not publish before his departure. See further Donna G. Cardamone, "The Salon as Marketplace in the 1550s: Patrons and Collectors of Lasso's Secular Music," in *Orlando di Lasso Studies,* ed. Peter Bergquist (Cambridge: Cambridge University Press, 1999), 64–90.

2. Fuller descriptions of all the sources are found in the critical report below.

3. Kristine K. Forney, "Orlando di Lasso's 'Opus 1': the Making and Marketing of a Renaissance Music Book," *Revue Belge de Musicologie* 39–40 (1985–86): 33–60. Donna G. Cardamone and David L. Jackson, "Multiple Formes and Vertical Setting in Susato's First Edition of Lassus's 'Opus 1'," *Music Library Association Notes* 46 (1989–90): 7–24, add considerable detail about Susato's printing process for these sources.

4. *CM 1,* xiii.

5. The discussion of the history of RISM 1555a/b is based on Forney, "Lasso's 'Opus 1'."

6. The dedication is transcribed in Forney on p. 58, with a translation on p. 37.

7. Cardamone assumes that all of Lasso's villanesche date from ca. 1550 to 1555; see her edition of Orlando di Lasso et al., *Canzoni Villanesche and Villanelle,* Recent Researches in the Music of the Renaissance, 82–83 (Madison: A-R Editions, 1991), xix.

8. Forney, 46–47, discusses the corrections in gathering A, which contains the madrigals, and provides an example.

9. Ibid., 51. Cardamone and Jackson, "Multiple Formes," especially pp. 20–21, discuss in detail the resetting of gathering E.

10. Boetticher, *Lasso,* 202 n. 4.

11. Ibid.

12. Boetticher, *Lasso,* 209, speculates that the designation "primo libro" implies a second book, which if it existed is completely lost. He believes that it would not have contained any Lasso motets that we do not know from other sources.

13. Boetticher, *Lasso,* 130.

14. Jacquet's motet is printed in Jacquet of Mantua, *Opera omnia,* ed. George Nugent and Philip Jackson (Rome: American Institute of Musicology; Neuhausen-Stuttgart: Hänssler, 1971–86), 4:9–15. James Erb discusses another early example of imitation or emulation, "Deliciae Phoebi," in *CM 1,* xvii.

15. Jacquet of Mantua, *Opera omnia,* 4:IX.

16. I have gathered information about other settings of the texts Lasso set from Harry B. Lincoln, *The Latin Motet: Indexes to Printed Collections, 1500–1600* (Ottawa: Institute of Medieval Music, 1993), work lists in *New Grove Dictionary of Music and Musicians, KBM5/1,* and references in the Lasso literature. I make no claim to absolute completeness.

17. Boetticher, *Lasso,* 130.

18. Ibid., 130, 246.

19. Jacobus Clemens non Papa, *Opera omnia,* ed. K.-P. Bernet Kempers (Rome: American Institute of Musicology, 1951–76), 20:54.

20. Boetticher, *Lasso,* 141.

21. Cardamone, "The Salon as Marketplace," 66.

22. Ignace Bossuyt, "Orlando di Lasso und Jean de Castro und ihre Beziehungen zu den italienischen humanistischen Kreisen in Antwerpen," paper delivered at a conference in Münster in 1998. I am grateful to Professor Bossuyt for sharing his paper with me before its publication.

23. Leuchtmann, *Leben,* 124–29, and Reinhold Schlötterer, *SWNR 21,* IX–XIII, offer convincing arguments for this dating. Boetticher, *Lasso,* 73–79, is one of a number of scholars who prefer an earlier date, based largely on stylistic or aesthetic grounds that are more subjective.

24. Edward E. Lowinsky, "Orlando di Lasso's Antwerp Motet Book," in *Music in the Culture of the Renaissance and Other Essays,* ed. Bonnie J. Blackburn, 2 vols. (Chicago: University of Chicago Press, 1989), 1:393 n. 48, and "Calmi sonum ferentes: A New Interpretation," ibid., 2:614.

25. David Crook, "Tonal Compass in the Motets of Orlando di Lasso," in *Hearing the Motet: Essays on the Motet*

of the Middle Ages and Renaissance, ed. Dolores Pesce (New York: Oxford University Press, 1997), 298–99.

26. A convenient summary of Latin contrafacta of Lasso's music and their publication histories may be found in Bernhold Schmid, "Zur Verbreitung lateinischer Kontrafakta nach Sätzen von Orlando di Lasso," *Musik in Bayern* 49 (1994), 5–17.

27. Lowinsky, "*Calami sonum ferentes*," 2:595–626.

28. Ibid., 610.

29. Boetticher, *Lasso*, 131.

30. Lowinsky, "*Calami sonum ferentes*," 2:612–16.

31. Bossuyt, "Orlando di Lasso und Jean de Castro."

32. E.g., "Quis mihi, quis tete rapuit," *CM 4*, 136–44; "Beatus ille qui procul negotiis," *CM 7*, 14–23.

33. Helmuth Osthoff, "Vergils Aeneis in der Musik von Josquin des Prez bis Orlando di Lasso," *Archiv für Musikwissenschaft* 11 (1954), 85–94. He cites settings by Josquin des Prez, Jean Verbonet [Johannes Ghiselin], Jean Mouton, Marbriano de Orto, Adrian Willaert, and several anonymous composers.

34. Willaert's motet is published in his *Opera omnia*, ed. Hermann Zenck et al. (Rome: American Institute of Musicology, 1950–), 2:59.

35. The contrafactum appears in *CM 6*, 171–79. Whether or not Lasso had anything to do with the substitute text is discussed *CM 6*, xv, xxi.

36. Schmid, "Verbreitung," 9, does not mention the inclusion of "Alma Venus" in the *Mellange* series.

37. Boetticher, *Lasso*, 128.

38. Ibid., 130. Because of the association he makes between the two motets, Boetticher dates "Alma Venus" prior to Lasso's move to Munich. This could be true, but no objective grounds support such a dating.

39. *CM 6*, xv. I am grateful to Bernhold Schmid for helping me to correct this error (personal communication, 30 July 1998).

40. "Vnd ist mir das Subiectum, darauf sie gesetzt, gleichwol In den oren geklungen, ich habs aber so bald nitt ertkhennen künden. Volgends als ich darnach gesungen, befind ich, das der Rö. M. Cappellmaister die selb auf das Tityre tu patulae, so der Orlando gemacht, componiert; wann ich dann wesst, das E.F.G. die selb nitt hätt, wolt ich sehen das Ich Ir die selb zuschicket. Glaub gentzlich sie würd Ir nitt so gar missfallen." Extracts from the original letter are published in Adolf Sandberger, *Beiträge zur Geschichte der bayerischen Hofkapelle unter Orlando di Lasso* (Leipzig: Breitkopf & Härtel, 1895), 3:303–4. The translation is from Milton Steinhardt, *Jacobus Vaet and His Motets* (East Lansing: Michigan State College Press, 1951), 10. Steinhardt's translation interpolates the word "motet" rather than "mass," suggesting that Albrecht was unacquainted with Lasso's motet. Seld clearly refers to the mass as "sie" and "die selb," and when he goes on to say "E.F.G. die selb nitt hatt," this also must refer to the mass rather than "das" Tityre, tu patulae. I am grateful to David Crook for drawing my attention to Steinhardt's misreading.

41. "Vnd sollen E.F.G. wissen, das der Rö. M. Capellmaister ain Motet mitt 6 gemacht, nemlich Vitam quam faciunt beatiorem, darinnen hatt er des Orlando Tityre tu patulae wellen Imitiren. Also ist die Mess auf beide die selben Moteten gemacht. Und schick derhalben E.F.G. das gemelt Vitam quam faciunt darzu." Text and translation from the sources cited in the preceding note; Steinhardt does not make clear that he quotes from two different letters. Vaet's motet is published in *Jacobus Vaet, Sämtliche Werke III*, ed. Milton Steinhardt, Denkmäler der Tonkunst in Österreich, 103–4 (Graz

and Vienna: Akademische Druck- und Verlagsanstalt, 1963), 139. His *Missa Tityre, tu patulae* is published in *Jacobus Vaet, Sämtliche Werke V*, ed. Milton Steinhardt, Denkmäler der Tonkunst in Österreich, 113–14 (Graz and Vienna: Akademische Druck- und Verlagsanstalt, 1965), 3, and his *Missa Vitam quae faciunt beatiorem* is published ibid., 44.

42. Boetticher, *Lasso*, 201 n. 3.

43. Mm. 10–13 of Lasso may be echoed in mm. 5–7 of Vaet, also mm. 64–67 (Lasso) and mm. 60–62 (Vaet).

44. Boetticher, *Lasso*, 231.

45. See the convenient summary by Albert Dunning in *New Grove Dictionary of Music and Musicians*, s.v. "Musica reservata (1)."

46. Boetticher, *Lasso*, 123.

47. Ibid.

48. Ibid., 103, 345–46.

49. Noel O'Regan, "Orlando di Lasso and Rome: Personal Contacts and Musical Influences," in *Orlando di Lasso Studies*, 140.

50. The setting in *Lectiones* is the third part of *Lectio* 8 and may be seen in Lasso, *Two Motet Cycles for Matins for the Dead*, ed. Peter Bergquist, Recent Researches in the Music of the Renaissance, 55 (Madison: A-R Editions, 1983), 70–73, and in *SWNR 19*, 86–90.

51. Bernhold Schmid, "Lasso's 'Fertur in conviviis:' on the History of its Text and Transmission," *Orlando di Lasso Studies*, 116–31. Unless otherwise stated, the following discussion of this motet is drawn from Schmid's study, which I am grateful to have had access to before its publication.

52. James Haar, "Lasso as Historicist," in *Hearing the Motet*, 272.

53. These settings printed respectively in Clemens, *Opera omnia*, 9:1; Willaert, *Opera omnia*, 5:154 (six voices); Thomas Crecquillon, *Opera omnia*, ed. Barton Hudson et. al. (Rome: American Institue of Musicology, 1974–), 12:103; *Treize livres de motets parus chez Pierre Attaignant*, ed. Albert Smijers (Monaco: Editions de l'Oiseau Lyre, 1936), 2:141. "Pater, peccavi" in *Liber Responsorialis* (Solesmes: Sancti Petri, 1895), 407, also includes a doxology, which is absent in all the polyphonic settings. Boetticher, *Lasso*, 217, finds similarities between Lasso's motet and an as yet unpublished four-voice setting by Willaert.

54. Rore's motet is printed in his *Opera omnia*, ed. Bernhard and Helga Meier (Rome: American Institute of Musicology, 1959–), 1:86.

55. "Orlando di Lasso and Andrea Gabrieli: Two Motets and Their Masses in a Munich Choirbook from 1564–65," in *Orlando di Lasso Studies*, 21. I am grateful to Professor Göllner for sharing with me her transcription of Gabrieli's as yet unpublished motet.

56. Further on Goulart's editions of the chansons see Richard Freeman, "Divins Accords: The Lassus Chansons and their Protestant Readers of the Late Sixteenth Century," *Orlandus Lassus and His Time*, Colloquium Proceedings, Antwerpen 24–26.08.1994, ed. Ignace Bossuyt et al. (Peer: Alamire, 1995), 273–94.

57. The structure of a collect is described in sources such as *The New Schaff-Herzog Encyclopedia of Religious Knowledge*, ed. Samuel Macauley Jackson (New York: Funk and Wagnalls, 1908–12), s. v. "Collect," and *The Oxford Dictionary of the Christian Church*, 3d ed., ed. E. A. Livingstone (Oxford University Press, 1997), s. v. "Collect." Both sources mention also the normal conclusion that pleads the merits of Christ, which understandably is omitted from "Deus qui bonum vinum creasti."

58. Personal communication, November 1997.

59. Boetticher, *Lasso*, 207–8, says that RISM 1566[17] is dedicated to the Duchess of Parma, then a few lines later says that he could not extract a dedication text from the fragmentary copy in Modena, Biblioteca Estense. He seemingly was not aware of the complete copy of the book in the British Library. On p. 166 he states that Rore dedicated the book to the *Duke* of Parma and that the inclusion of Lasso's motet suggests a friendship between Rore and Lasso. The confusion seems to have arisen from Boetticher's lack of access to the complete copy of the book and its dedication. Rore did not dedicate the posthumous publication, and Gardano's dedication clearly speaks of Rore as deceased. Bernhard Meier called attention to Boetticher's confusion in his preface to Rore, *Opera omnia*, 5:ix; that volume includes a facsimile of Gardano's dedication on p. xix.

60. Giulio M. Ongaro, "Venetian Printed Anthologies of Music in the 1560s and the Role of the Editor," *The Dissemination of Music*, ed. Hans Lenneberg (London: Gordon and Breach, 1994), 50. I am grateful to Professor Ongaro for providing me with a copy of his article.

61. *CM 5*, xi and plate 2.

62. Boetticher, *Lasso*, 226.

63. Ibid., 219.

64. *Drei Motetten über den Text Quem dicunt homines*, ed. Lewis Lockwood, Das Chorwerk, 94 (Wolfenbüttel: Möseler, 1963).

65. Boetticher, *Lasso*, 237–39.

66. Marie Louise Göllner, "Lassos Motetten nach Hymnentexten und ihre Parodiemessen von Ivo de Vento und Andrea Gabrieli," *Orlando di Lasso in der Musikgeschichte. Bericht über das Symposion der Bayerischen Akademie der Wissenschaften, München, 4.–6. Juli 1994*, ed. Bernhold Schmid (Munich: Verlag der Bayerischen Akademie der Wissenschaften, 1996), 87–100.

67. Munich, Bayerische Staatsbibliothek, Mus. Ms. 17; see *KBM5/1*, 85.

68. Printed with modern German translations in Horst Leuchtmann, *Orlando di Lasso: Briefe* (Wiesbaden: Breitkopf und Härtel, 1977).

69. Boetticher, *Lasso*, 233–34.

70. *SWNR 1*, 1*–8*.

71. Ibid., VII*.

72. See *CM 5*, xvi–xix. Those motets are "Zachaee, festinans descende" and "Gloria Patri."

73. Boetticher, *Lasso*, 357. On p. 350 he questions why Gerlach did not include "Laetentur caeli" and "Fratres, sobrii estote" in RISM 1568b, suggesting that these and other four-voice motets appeared earlier, most likely in a hypothetical lost Scotto edition he would date at 1564 (351 n. 47). This discussion is confused because Boetticher in n. 47 uses the siglum 1564*v* to refer to the supposed Scotto print, but on p. 753 and elsewhere the same siglum designates a supposed Susato print. In the absence of solid evidence it is difficult to accept Boetticher's speculations about lost printed sources.

Texts and Translations

The orthography of the Latin texts has been normalized in accordance with the Editio Vaticana or Vulgate for liturgical and biblical texts and a standard Latin dictionary for other texts (Charlton T. Lewis and Lewis Short, *A Latin Dictionary*, 1879; reprint, Oxford: Clarendon Press, 1958). When the Editio Vaticana and Vulgate differ in punctuation and in their numeration of psalm verses, the former has been preferred. Translations of biblical texts are from the Douay-Rheims Bible, slightly modified in a few places to express better the sense of the Latin in modern English; all other translations are by the present editor except as noted.

1. *Audi dulcis amica mea*

Audi dulcis amica mea, auribus percipe verba oris mei. Nigra es sed formosa, et macula non est in te, ideo amore tuo langueo, et quia tribulor ad te confugio. Exaudi deprecor orationem meam.

Hearken, my sweet beloved, hear with your ears the words of my mouth. Thou art black but comely, and there is no spot in thee, therefore I am faint from your love, and because I am afflicted I take refuge with you. Hear my plea, I beg.

Comment: The text is conflated from verses from Song of Sol., including 1:4, 2:5, 4:7.

2. *Peccantem me quotidie*

Peccantem me quotidie, et non me paenitentem, timor mortis conturbat me: Quia in inferno nulla est redemptio, miserere mei Deus, et salva me.

Since I sin daily and am not penitent, the fear of death confounds me: because in hell there is no redemption, have mercy on me, God, and save me.

Comment: Responsory 7, Office for the Dead, respond only.

3. *Inclina Domine aurem tuam*

Inclina Domine aurem tuam et exaudi me: quoniam inops et pauper sum ego.
Laetifica animam servi tui, quoniam ad te Domine animam meam levavi.

Incline thy ear, O Lord, and hear me: for I am needy and poor.
Give joy to the soul of thy servant, for to thee, O Lord, I have lifted up my soul.

(Ps. 85:1, 3b)

Comment: This text corresponds partially to the Introit for the Fifteenth Sunday after Pentecost, which uses Ps. 85:1a and 2b–3a for its antiphon section and 3b for its verse.

4. Domine, quando veneris (1)

Domine, quando veneris judicare terram, ubi me abscondam a vultu irae tuae? Quia peccavi nimis in vita mea.

Lord, when you shall come to judge the earth, where shall I hide myself from the face of thy wrath? For I have sinned greatly in my life.

Comment: Responsory 3, Office for the Dead, respond only.

5. Alma Nemes

Alma Nemes, quae sola Nemes, quae dicere Cypris
   altera, quae Pallas altera, quarta Charis,

quae pellis nubes, quae caelum fronte serenas

   et risu et laetis flammea luminibus,
alma veni vocemque tuam, qua flumina sistis

   funde, canas mecum dulce novumque melos.
       (Lasso? Stefano Ambrosio Schiappalaria?)

Propitious Nemes, you who are the one-and-only Nemes,
   who are called a second Venus, a second Minerva, a
   fourth Grace,
you who dispels the clouds, who cheers heaven with
   your brow
   and the fiery orbs with your laughter and happy eyes,
come, kind one, and pour forth your voice,
   with which you make rivers stand still,
   sing with me a sweet, new song.

Comment: Elegiac couplets.

6. Calami sonum ferentes

Calami sonum ferentes Siculo leve numero

non pellunt gemitus pectore ab imo nimium graves:

nec qui strepente sunt ab Aufido revulsi.
Musa quae nemus incolis Sirmionis amoenum,
reddita qua lenis, Lesbia dura fuit;
me adi recessu principis mei tristem.
Musa deliciae tui Catulli
dulce tristibus his tuum junge carmen avenis.
       (Giovanni Battista Pigna [1530–75])

The reed-pipes giving forth a sound in light Sicilian
   meter
Do not banish the sighs, all too painful, from the depth
   of my heart.
Nor do those [reeds] plucked from the roaring Aufidus.
O Muse, who dwell'st in the pleasant groves of Sirmio,
Through whom unfeeling Lesbia grew tender,
Visit me, who mourn the departure of my prince.
O Muse, delight of thy Catullus,
Join thy sweet song to the sad [sound of my] pipes.

Comment: The poem is entitled "Fistula tertia ex Catulli numeris" in Pigna's Carminum libri quatuor (Venice: Vincentius Valgrisium, 1553), 99. The poem and its translation are both taken from Edward E. Lowinsky, "Calami sonum ferentes: A New Interpretation," in Music in the Culture of the Renaissance and Other Essays, ed. Bonnie J. Blackburn, 2 vols. (Chicago: University of Chicago Press, 1989), 2:608, and are used by permission of the publisher.

7. Dulces exuviae

"Dulces exuviae, dum fata deusque sinebat,
accipite hanc animam meque his exsolvite curis.
Vixi et quem dederat cursum fortuna peregi,

et nunc magna mei sub terras ibit imago.

"Relics cherished so long as fate and the god permitted,
receive this spirit and release me from these cares;
I have lived, and I have completed the course fortune
   gave me,
and now my noble shade will pass beneath the earth.

Secunda pars
"Urbem praeclaram statui, mea moenia vidi,
ulta virum poenas inimico ab hoste recepi,

Second part
"I founded a splendid city, I have seen my bulwarks,
avenged my husband, received satisfaction from a
   hostile foe,

felix, heu nimium felix, si littora tantum
nunquam Dardaniae tetigissent nostra carinae."
Dixit, et os impressa toro, "Moriemur inultae,

sed moriamur" ait. "Sic, sic juvat ire sub umbras."

happy, alas all too happy, if only the Trojan
keels had never touched our shores."
She spoke, and pressing her face to the couch. "we shall
die unavenged,
but let us die," she said. "Thus, thus I am happy to go
down to the shades below."

(Virgil *Aeneid* 4.651–60)

Comment: Virgil in line 656 has "a fratre" rather than "ab hoste."

8. Alma Venus

Alma Venus vultu languentem despice laeto,

Respice languentem dulciter alma Venus.
Anni principio tibi prospera cuncta precamur,

Ut placida subeat pectore noster amor

Et mihi fausta satis fuerint haec omnia Iani
Annua qui nobis lumina laeta refert.
Alma Venus, etc.

Propitious Venus, look down to the weary one with a
happy countenance,
regard the weary one favorably, propitious Venus.
At the beginning of the year we entreat all good fortune from you,
that [you being] gentle, our love may rise from the
heart.
And that all these annual observances of Janus,
who brings us happy days, be favorable to me.
Propitious Venus, etc.

Secunda pars
Nunc elegos divae quaerulos dimittere versus.

Undique solicitis resoluto pectore curis,

Musica nunc alio demulceat omnia cantu,
Protinus ex misero videor dum maximus heros.

Nam mea me placidis oculis respexit amica
Et poenitus nostro delevit corde dolorem.

Second part
Now is the time to leave off the plaintive elegiac verses
of the goddess.
My heart having been entirely released from worrisome cares,
let music now ease everything with another song,
while I seem from [having been] a wretch now the
mightiest hero.
For now my love looks on me with calm eyes,
and drives away sorrow completely from my breast.

Comment: Elegiac couplets.

9. Tityre, tu patulae

Tityre, tu patulae recubans sub tegmine fagi,
Sylvestrem tenui Musam meditaris avena.
Nos patriae fines et dulcia linquimus arva.
Nos patriam fugimus; tu, Tityre, lentus in umbra
Formosam resonare doces Amarillida silvas.

Tityrus, you lie beneath the spreading beech
and practice country songs upon a slender pipe.
I leave my father's fields and my sweet ploughlands,
an exile from my native soil. You sprawl in the shade
and school the woods to sound with Amaryllis's charms.

Secunda pars
O Meliboee, deus nobis haec otia fecit.
Namque erit ille mihi semper deus, illius aram
Saepe tener nostris ab ovilibus imbuet agnus.
Ille meas errare boves, ut cernis, et ipsum
Ludere quae vellem calamo permisit agresti.

Second part
O Meliboeus, it was a god who gave me this repose.
He'll always be a god to me. Often I'll stain
his altar with blood of a young lamb from my fold. He
it was who allowed my cattle to graze like this and me
to play the songs I choose upon my rustic flute.

(Virgil *Eclogues* 1.1–10)

Comment: The translation by Barbara Hughes Fowler from *Vergil's Eclogues* (Chapel Hill: University of North Carolina Press, 1997) is used by permission of the publisher.

10. Quia vidisti me, Thoma

Quia vidisti me, Thoma, credidisti: beati qui non viderunt, et crediderunt, alleluia.

(John 20:29)

Because thou hast seen me, Thomas, thou hast believed: blessed are they that have not seen, and have believed, alleluia.

Comment: Antiphon for the Magnificat and Benedictus, feast of St. Thomas.

11. Scio enim quod redemptor meus vivit

Scio enim quod redemptor meus vivit, et in novissimo die de terra surrecturus sum; [et] rursum circumdabor pelle mea, et in carne mea videbo Deum salvatorem meum.

(Job 19:25–26)

For I know that my Redeemer liveth, and in the last day I shall rise out of the earth. And I shall be clothed again with my skin, and in my flesh I shall see God my savior.

Comment: This text, somewhat altered, is Responsory 1, Office for the Dead, respond only.

12. Fertur in conviviis

Fertur in conviviis vinus, vina, vinum;
masculinum displicet atque foemininum,
sed in neutro genere vinum est divinum.
Loqui facit clericum optimum latinum.

In banquets is served he-wine, she-wine, it-wine;
the masculine displeases, also the feminine,
but in the neuter gender wine is divine.
It makes the clerics speak in the best Latin.

Volo inter omnia vinum pertransire.
Vinum facit vetulas leviter salire
et ditescit pauperes, claudos facit ire,
mutis dat eloquium, surdisque audire.

I want wine to be everywhere.
Wine makes the old women jump agilely,
and it makes paupers grow rich, the lame walk,
it gives the mute eloquence and makes the deaf hear.

Potatores inclyti semper sunt benigni,
tam senes quam juvenes. In aeterno igni
cruciantur rustici qui non sunt tam digni
ut gustare valeant boni haustum vini.

Celebrated drinkers are always benign,
the old as well as the young. In the eternal fire
are tortured the boors who are not so worthy
that they deserve to take a swallow of good wine.

Meum est propositum in taberna mori
et vinum apponere sitientiori,
ut dicant cum venerint angelorum chori,

Deus sit propitius huic potatori.

My intention is to die in the tavern
and serve the wine to a thirstier one,
so that when the choruses of angels shall come they may say,
God be gracious to this drinker.

Et plus quam ecclesiam diligo tabernum,
illum nullo tempore sprevi neque spernam,
donec sanctos angelos venientes cernam
cantantes pro ebriis, "Requiem aeternam."

And more than the church I love the tavern,
at no time have I spurned nor will I spurn it,
until I see the holy angels coming
singing for the drunkards, "Requiem aeternam."

13. Quid prodest stulto

Quid prodest stulto habere divitias, cum sapientiam emere non possit? Qui altam facit domum suam, quaerit ruinam, et qui evitat discere incidit in malum.

Qui perversi cordis est, non invenit bonum. Vanitas vanitatum, et omnia vanitas.
Tenor 1: Vanitas vanitatum, et omnia vanitas.

(Prov. 17:16, 20; Eccles. 1:2)

What doth it avail a fool to have riches, seeing he can not buy wisdom? He that maketh his house high, seeketh a downfall: and he that refuseth to learn, shall fall into evils.

He that is of a perverse heart, shall not find good. Vanity of vanities, and all is vanity.
Tenor 1: Vanity of vanities, and all is vanity.

14. Pater, peccavi

Pater, peccavi in caelum, et coram te: jam non sum dignus vocari filius tuus: Fac me sicut unum ex mercenariis tuis.

Secunda pars

Quanti mercenarii in domo patris mei abundant panibus, ego autem hic fame pereo! Surgam, et ibo ad patrem meum, et dicam ei: Fac me sicut unum ex mercenariis tuis.

(Luke 15:18b–19, 17b–18)

Father, I have sinned against heaven, and before thee: I am not worthy to be called thy son: make me as one of thy hired servants.

Second part

How many hired servants in my father's house abound with bread, and I here perish with hunger? I will arise, and will go to my father, and say to him: make me as one of thy hired servants.

Comment: Responsory 1, Saturday before the Third Sunday of Lent.

15. Deus qui bonum vinum creasti

Deus qui bonum vinum creasti,
et ex eodem multa capita dolere fecisti,
da nobis quaesumus intellectum
ut saltem possimus invenire lectum

God who created good wine,
and by the same has made many heads ache,
grant us we pray the good sense
that we may at least be able to find our beds.

16. Forte soporifera

Forte soporifera ad baias dormivit in umbra

   Blandus amor, placuit plus ubi murmur aquae.
Flucticolae accurunt nymphae, nereia turba.
   Vindex ardoris vult fore quaeque sui.
Absconduntque facem sub aquis, quis crederet,

   Ecce parturit eternum mox liquor ille focum
Balnea perpetuo hinc fervent calefacta calore.
   Curatur nullis ardor amoris aquis.

By chance seductive Amor slept in the drowsy shade
   by the bays,
   where the murmur of the water was most pleasing.
The water-nymphs approached, the Nereid throng.
   Each one wants to be the advocate of her passion.
They hide a torch under the waters, so that he might
   believe them.
   Behold, soon water gives birth to the eternal fire,
The heated baths boil hereafter with perpetual heat.
   The ardor of love is soothed by no waters.

Comment: Elegiac couplets.

17. Quis est homo qui timet Dominum?

Quis est homo qui timet Dominum? legem statuit ei in via, quam elegit.
Anima ejus in bonis demorabitur: et semen ejus hereditabit terram.

(Ps. 24:12–13)

Who is the man that feareth the Lord? He hath appointed him a law in the way he hath chosen.
His soul shall dwell in good things: and his seed shall inherit the land.

18. Ubi est Abel

Ubi est Abel frater tuus? dixit Dominus ad Cain. Nescio, Domine, numquid custos fratris mei sum ego? Et dixit ad eum: Quid fecisti? Ecce vox sanguinis fratris tui Abel clamat ad me de terra.

(Gen. 4:9–10)

Where is thy brother Abel? said the Lord to Cain. I know not, Lord, am I my brother's keeper? And he said to him: What hast thou done? Behold, the voice of thy brother's blood crieth to me from the earth.

Comment: Responsory 9, Septuagesima, respond only.

19. *Quem dicunt homines*

Quem dicunt homines esse Filium hominis? dixit Jesus discipulis suis. Respondens Petrus, dixit:

Secunda pars
Tu es Christus Filius Dei vivi. Et ego dico tibi, quia tu es Petrus, et super hanc petram aedificabo Ecclesiam meam.

(Matt. 16:13, 16, 18)

Who do men say that the Son of man is? said Jesus to his disciples. Peter answering said:

Second part
Thou art Christ, the Son of the living God. And I say to thee: That thou art Peter, and upon this rock I will build my church.

Comment: Responsory, feasts of St. Peter, respond only.

20. *Jesu, nostra redemptio*

Jesu, nostra redemptio,
amor et desiderium,
Deus Creator omnium,
homo in fine temporum:
    Quae te vicit clementia,
ut ferres nostra crimina,
crudelem mortem patiens,
ut nos a morte tolleres.

Secunda pars
    Inferni claustra penetrans,
tuos captivos redimens,
victor triumpho nobili
ad dextram Dei residens.

Tertia pars
    Ipsa te cogat pietas,
ut mala nostra superes
parcendo, et voti compotes
nos tuo vultu saties.

Quarta pars
    Tu esto nostrum gaudium,
qui es futurus praemium:
sit nostra in te gloria
in sempiterna saecula. Amen.

Jesus, our redemption,
love and desire,
God, the creator of all,
for man at the end of time:
    What clemency has conquered thee,
that thou shouldst bear our crimes,
suffering cruel death
that thou might remove us from death.

Second part
    Breaching the gates of hell,
redeeming thy captives,
the victor in noble triumph
residing at the right hand of the Father.

Third part
    May piety itself contrain thee
that, having mercy on our ills, thou may
triumph, and with vows satisfied
thou may satisfy us with thy face.

Fourth part
    Be thou our joy,
who art the reward to come:
may our glory be towards thee
for all time to come. Amen.

Comment: Hymn, Ascension. In Editio Vaticana the last line reads: "per cuncta semper saecula."

1. *S, U, su, P, E, R, per*

S, U, su, P, E, R, per, super,
F, L, U, flu, per flu, super flu,
M, I, mi, flumi, per flumi, super flumi,
N, A, na, mina, flumina, per flumina, super flumina,
B, A, ba, na ba, mina ba, flumina ba, per flumina ba,
    super flumina ba,
B, I, bi, babi, na babi, mina babi, flumina babi, per flumina babi, super flumina babi,
L, O, lo, bilo, babilo, na babilo, mina babilo, flumina babilo, per flumina babilo, super flumina babilo,
N, I, S, nis, lonis, bilonis, Babilonis, na Babilonis, mina Babilonis, flumina Babilonis, per flumina Babilonis, super flumina Babilonis.

By the rivers of Babylon.

Secunda pars

I, L, il, L, I, C, lic, illic,

S, E, se, lic se, illic se,

D, I, di, sedi, lic sedi, illic sedi,

M, U, S, mus, dimus, sedimus, lic sedimus, illic sed-
    imus,

E, T, et, mus et, dimus et, sedimus et, lic sedimus et,
    illic sedimus et,

F, L, E, fle, et fle, mus et fle, dimus et fle, sedimus et
    fle, lic sedimus et fle, illic sedimus et fle,

V, I, vi, flevi, et flevi, mus et flevi, dimus et flevi, sed-
    imus et flevi, lic sedimus et flevi, illic sedimus et
    flevi,

M, U, S, mus, vimus, flevimus, et flevimus, mus et fle-
    vimus, dimus et flevimus, sedimus et flevimus,
    lic sedimus et flevimus, illic sedimus et flevimus.

(Ps. 136:1a)

Second part

There we sat and wept.

22. *Audi, benigne conditor*

Audi, benigne conditor,
nostras preces cum fletibus,
in hoc sacro jejunio
fusas quadragenario.
    Scrutator alme cordium,
infirma tu scis virium:
ad te reversis exhibe
remissionis gratiam.

Hear, kind creator,
our pleas with tears,
in this sacred fasting time
spread over forty days.
    Nourishing examiner of hearts,
thou knowest the weaknesses of men:
show thy grace through
returning pardon.

Secunda pars

Multum quidem peccavimus,
poenasque comparavimus,
sed cuncta, qui solus potes,
confer medelam languidis.
    Sic corpus extra conteri
dona per abstinentiam:
jejunet ut mens sobria
a labe prorsus criminum.

(Attributed to St. Gregory the Great)

Second part

We have sinned greatly indeed,
and we have received punishment,
but bestow, as thou only art able,
on all things the remedy of the feeble.
    Allow thus the body to be chastised
without by abstinence:
let it fast so that the sober mind
from the destruction of sin truly [escapes].

Comment: Hymn, Lent. Lasso set only four of the hymn's five strophes. His third and
fourth strophes are different from Editio Vaticana, which reads: "Multum quidem pec-
cavimus, | sed parce confitentibus: | ad laudem tui nominis | confer medelam languidis.
| Concede nostrum conteri | corpus per abstinentiam, | culpae ut relinquant pabulum |
jejuna corda criminum." Lasso's version is found in a 1556 collection of hymns by
Georgius Cassandrus; see Philip Wackernagel, *Das deutsche Kirchelied*, 5 vols. (Leipzig:
Teubner, 1864–77), 1:73, no. 100.

23. *Domine, quando veneris (2)*

See no. 4 above for text and translation.

24. *Tribulationem et dolorem inveni*

Tribulationem et dolorem inveni: et nomen Domini
    invocavi.
O Domine libera animam meam: misericors Dominus
    et justus, et Deus noster miseretur.

I met with trouble and sorrow: and I called upon the
    name of the Lord.
O Lord, deliver my soul. The Lord is merciful and
    just, and our God sheweth mercy.

Secunda pars
Convertere animam meam in requiem tuam: quia
    Dominus benefecit tibi.
Quia eripuit animam meam de morte: oculos meos a
    lacrimis, pedes meos a lapsu.

(Ps. 114:4–5, 7–8)

Second part
Turn my soul into thy rest: for the Lord hath been
    bountiful to thee.
For he hath delivered my soul from death: my eyes
    from tears, my feet from falling.

Comment: V. 7 in Vulgate and Editio Vaticana begins: "Convertere, anima mea."

25. *Laetentur caeli*

Laetentur caeli, et exsultet terra: commoveatur mare,
    et plenitudo ejus: gaudebunt campi, et omnia
    quae in eis sunt.

Let the heavens rejoice, and let the earth be glad, let
    the sea be moved, and the fulness thereof; the
    fields and all things that are in them shall be joyful.

Secunda pars
Tunc exsultabunt omnia ligna silvarum a facie Domini,
    quia venit: quoniam venit judicare terram.

(Ps. 95:11–12)

Second part
Then shall all the trees of the woods rejoice before the
    face of the Lord, because he cometh: because he
    cometh to judge the earth.

26. *Fratres, sobrii estote*

Fratres, sobrii estote, et vigilate: quia adversarius vester
    diabolus tamquam leo rugiens circuit, quaerens
    quem devoret: cui resistite fortes in fide.

(I Peter 5:8–9)

Brothers, be sober and watch: because your adversary
    the devil, as a roaring lion, goeth about seeking
    whom he may devour. Whom resist ye, strong in
    faith.

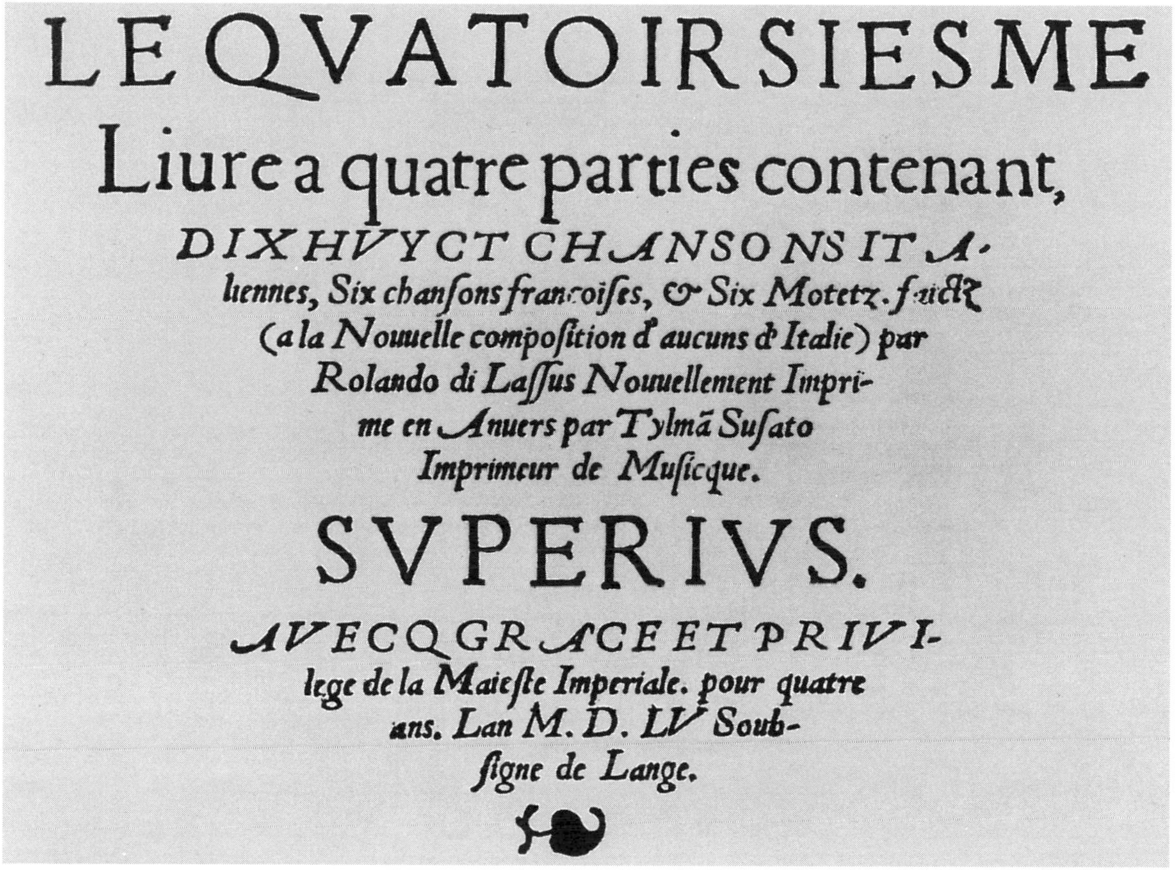

LE QVATOIRSIESME
Liure a quatre parties contenant,
DIX HVYCT CHANSONS ITA-
liennes, Six chansons francoises, & Six Motetz. fuict
(a la Nouuelle compofition d'aucuns d'Italie) par
Rolando di Laſſus Nouuellement Impri-
me en Anuers par Tylmã Suſato
Imprimeur de Muſicque.

SVPERIVS.
AVECQ GRACE ET PRIVI-
lege de la Maieſte Imperiale. pour quatre
ans. Lan M. D. LV Soub-
figne de Lange.

Plate 1. Orlando di Lasso, *Le quatoirsiesme Livre a quatre parties* (Antwerp: Susato, 1555), Superius partbook, title page (courtesy of Musikabteilung, Bayerische Staatsbibliothek, Munich)

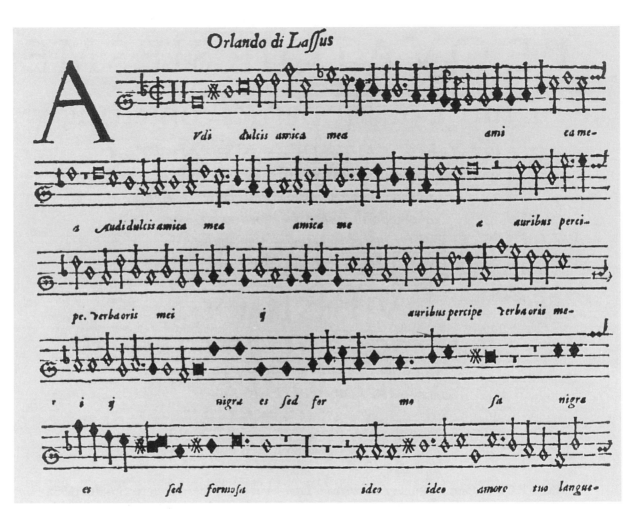

Plate 2. Orlando di Lasso, *Le quatoirsiesme Livre a quatre parties* (Antwerp: Susato, 1555), Superius partbook, "Audi dulcis amica mea," beginning, fol. 15v (courtesy of Musikabteilung, Bayerische Staatsbibliothek, Munich)

Plate 3. Munich, Bayerische Staatsbibliothek, Mus. Ms. 20, fols. 190v–191r, Orlando di Lasso, "Dulces exuviae," beginning (courtesy of Musikabteilung, Bayerische Staatsbibliothek, Munich)

1. Audi dulcis amica mea

-ris _____ me- i,⟩ au- ri- bus per- ci- pe ver- ba
__ me- i, ver- ba o- ris me- i, _____
-ri- bus per- ci- pe⟩ ver- ba o- ris me- i,
au- ri- bus per- ci- pe ver- ba

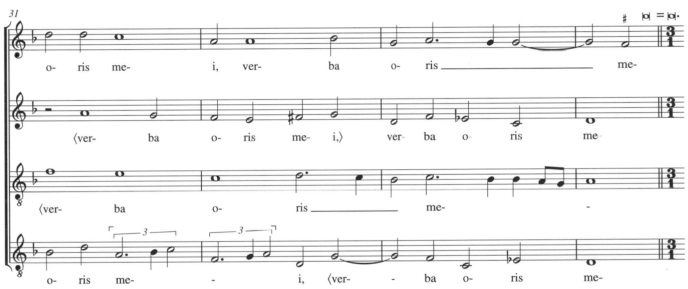

o- ris me- i, ver- ba o- ris _____ me-
⟨ver- ba o- ris me- i,⟩ ver- ba o- ris me-
⟨ver- ba o- ris _____ me- ᵃ
o- ris me- i, ⟨ver- ba o- ris me-

-i. Ni- gra es sed for- mo- sa,
-i. Ni- gra es sed for- mo-
-i.⟩ Ni- gra es _____ sed _____ for- mo- sa, ni- gra
-i.⟩ Ni- gra es sed for- mo- sa, ni- gra es, _____

2. Peccantem me quotidie

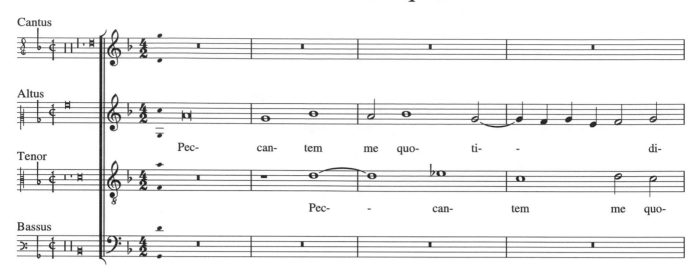

Cantus

Altus

Pec- can- tem me quo- ti- - di-

Tenor

Pec- - can- tem me quo-

Bassus

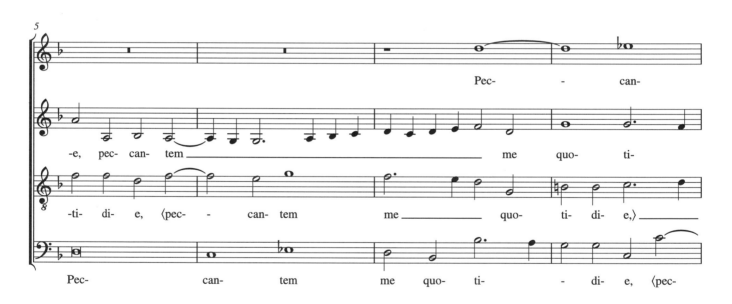

-e, pec can- tem _____ me quo- ti-

-ti- di- e, ⟨pec- - can- tem me _____ quo- ti- di- e,⟩ _____

Pec- can- tem me quo- ti- - di- e, ⟨pec-

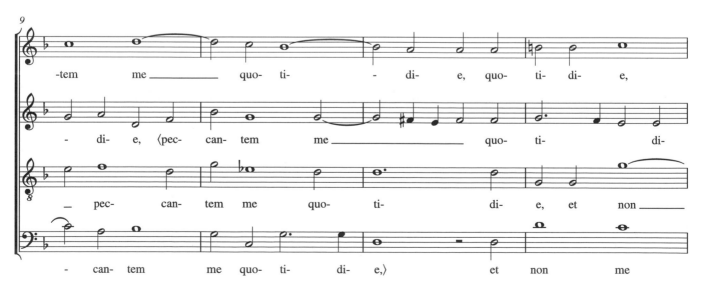

-tem me _____ quo- ti- - di- e, quo- ti- di- e,

- di- e, ⟨pec- can- tem me _____ quo- ti- di-

_ pec- can- tem me quo- ti- di- e, et non _____

- can- tem me quo- ti- di- e,⟩ et non me

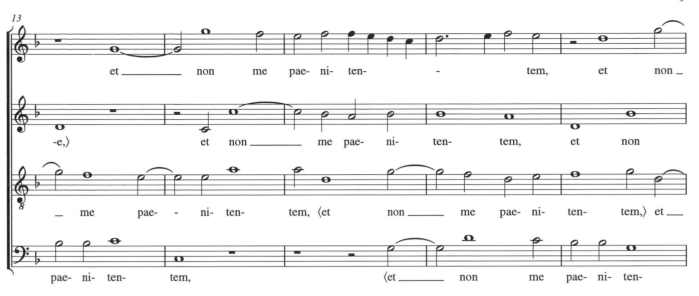

et ___ non me pae- ni- ten- - tem, et non ___
-e,⟩ et non ___ me pae- ni- ten- tem, et non
___ me pae- ni- ten- tem, ⟨et non ___ me pae- ni- ten- tem,⟩ et ___
pae- ni- ten- tem, ⟨et ___ non me pae- ni- ten-

___ me pae- ni ten- - tem, time [pae- ni- ten- tem,] ti- - mor mor-
___ non ___ me pae- ni- ten- - tem, ___ ti-
-tem,⟩ et non me pae- ni- ten- tem, ti- mor

- mor mor- - tis con- tur- bat ___ me, ⟨ti- mor mor- tis
- tis con- tur- bat me, ⟨ti- - mor mor- tis ___ con- tur-
- mor mor- tis con- tur- bat ___ me, con- tur- bat me, ti-
mor- - tis, ti- - mor mor- - tis con-

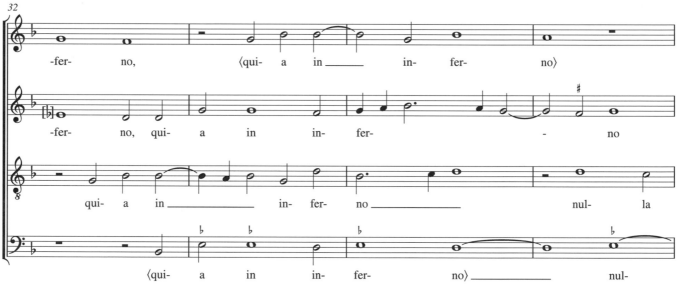

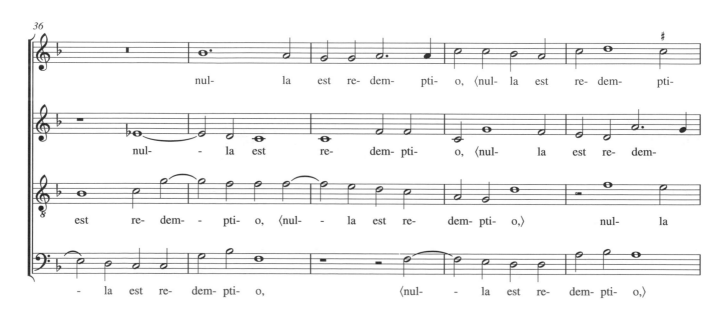

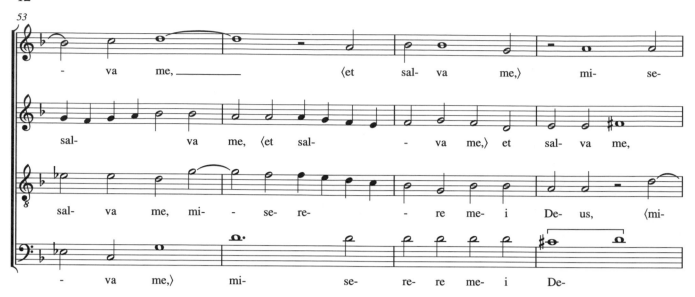

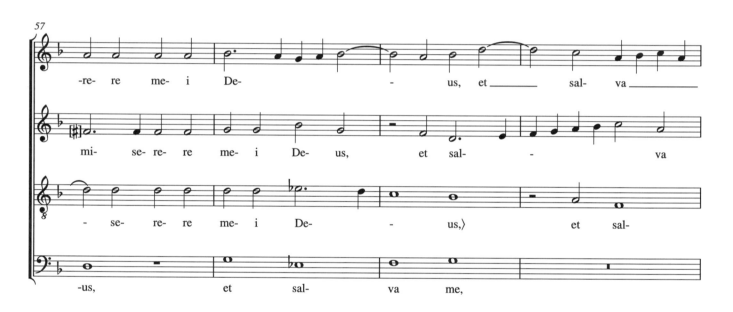

3. Inclina Domine aurem tuam

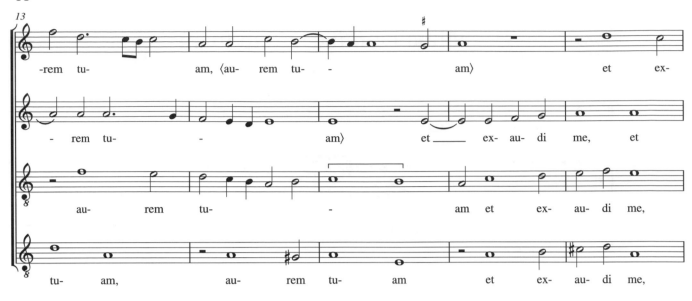

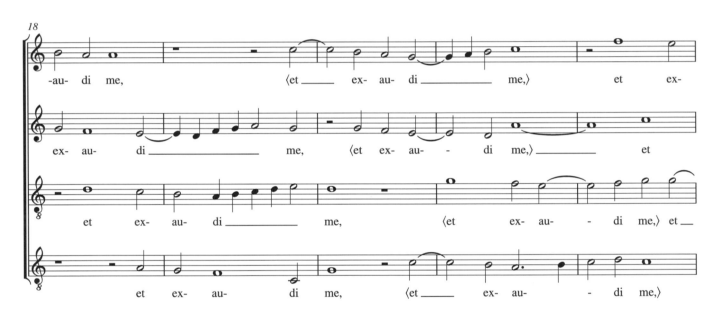

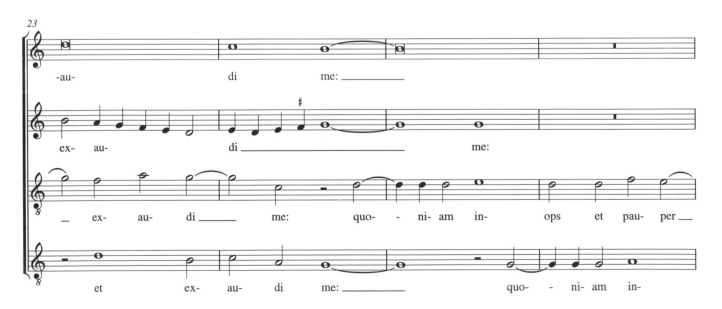

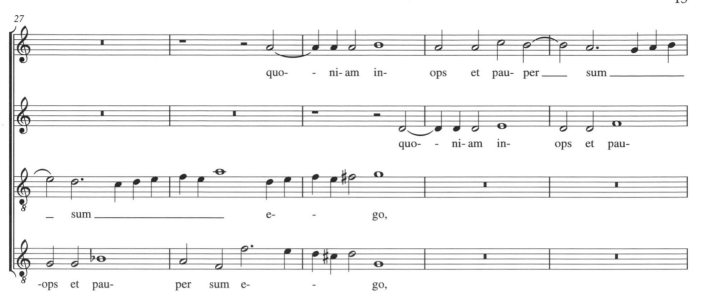

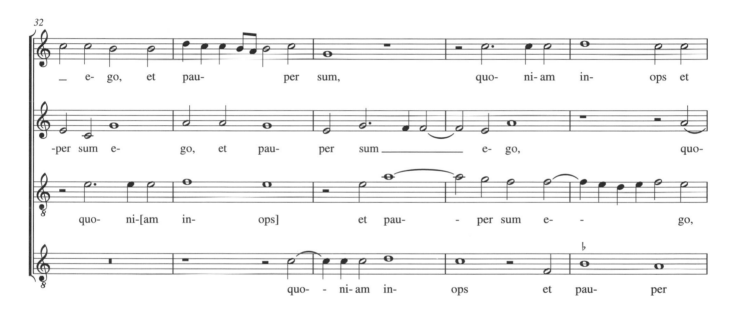

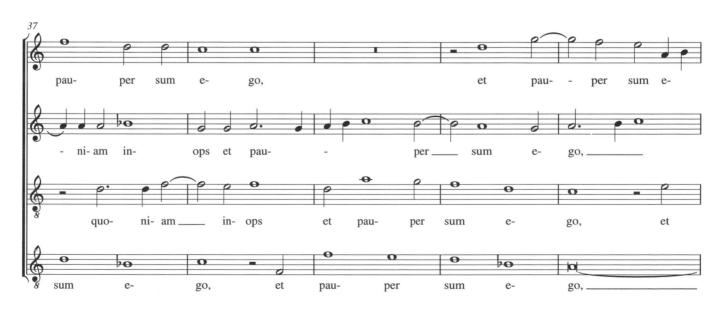

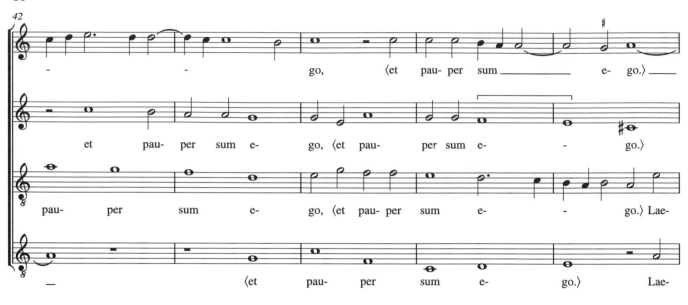

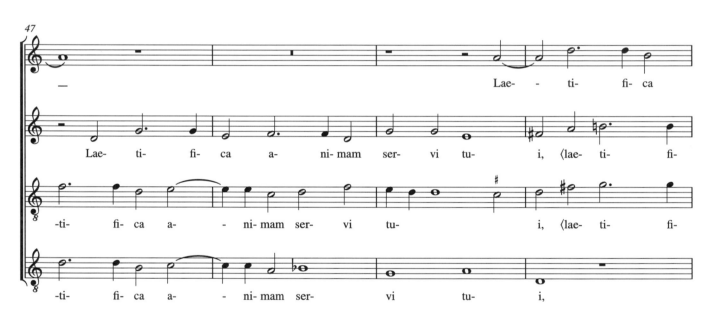

4. Domine, quando veneris (1)

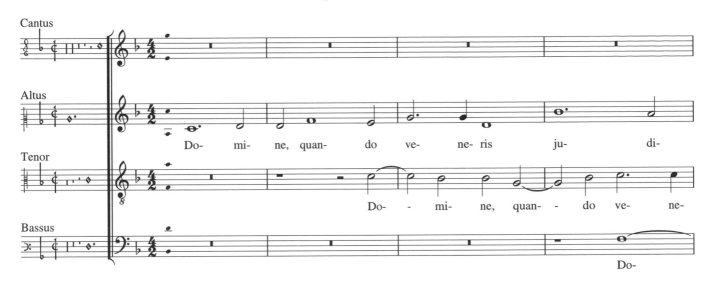

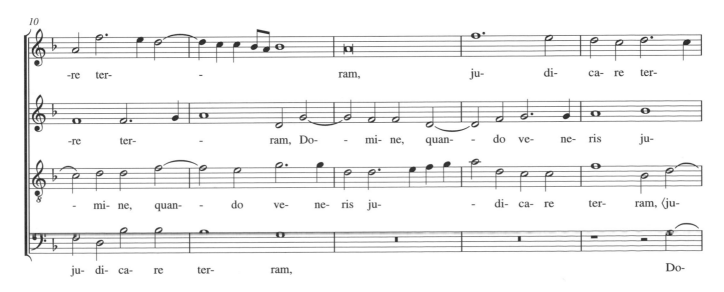

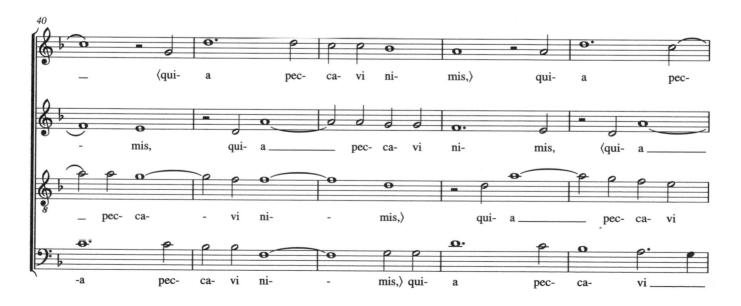

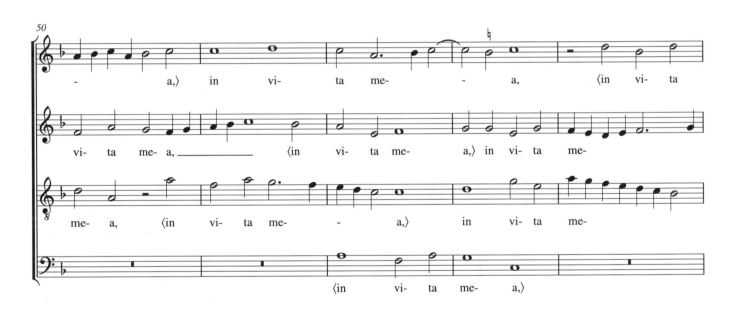

5. Alma Nemes

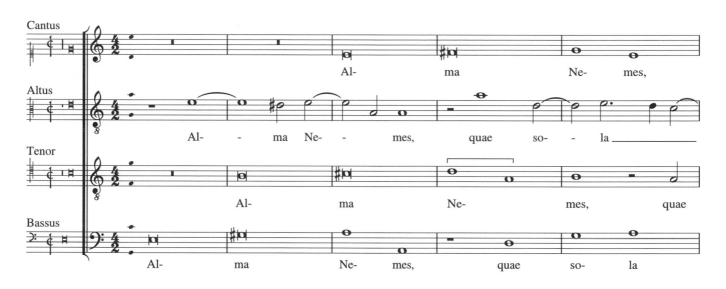

al- te- ra,⟩ quar- ta Cha- ris, quae _____ pel- lis nu-

- las al- - te- ra,⟩ quar- ta Cha- ris, _____ quae _____

- te- ra, quar- ta Cha- ris, quae pel- - lis nu-

quar- ta Cha- ris, quae pel- - lis nu-

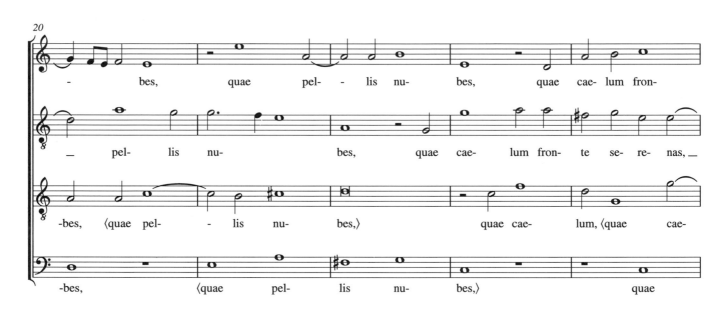

- bes, quae pel- - lis nu- bes, quae cae- lum fron-

_ pel- lis nu- bes, quae cae- lum fron- te se- re- nas, _

-bes, ⟨quae pel- - lis nu- bes,⟩ quae cae- lum, ⟨quae cae-

-bes, ⟨quae pel- lis nu- bes,⟩ quae

-te se- re- nas et ri- - su

_____ fron- te se- re- nas et ri- - su

- lum⟩ fron- te se- re- nas et ri-

cae- lum fron- te se- re- nas et ri-

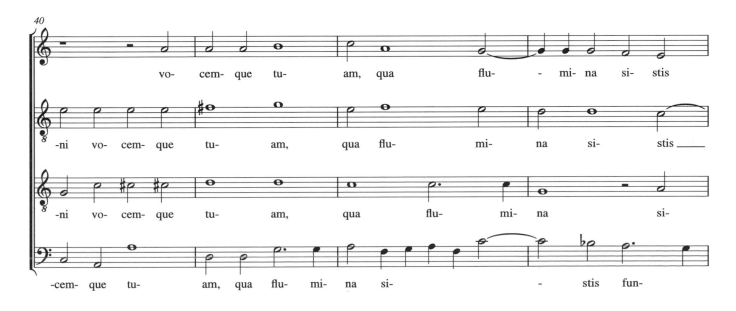

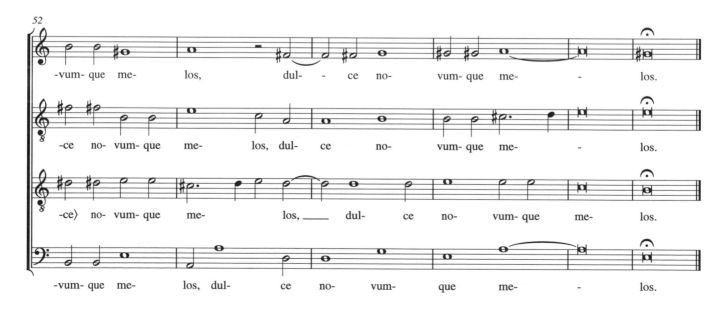

6. Calami sonum ferentes

Cipriano de Rore

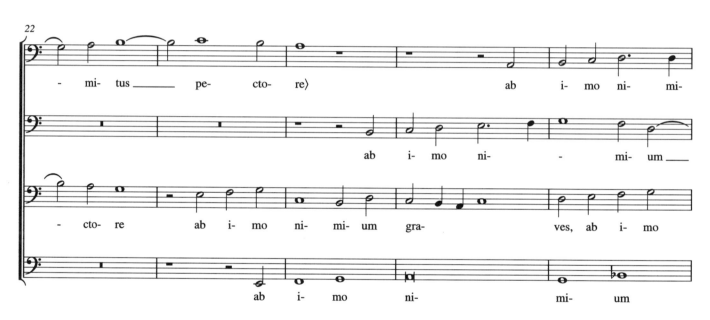

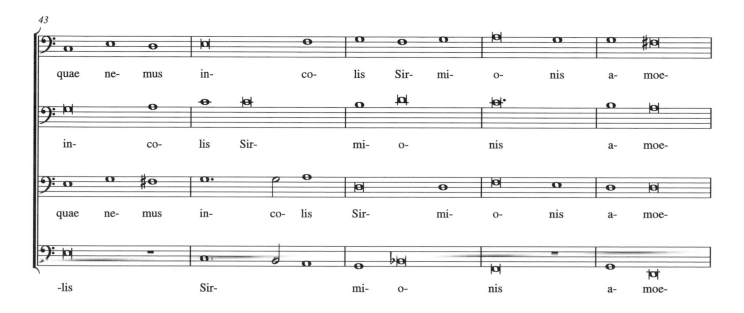

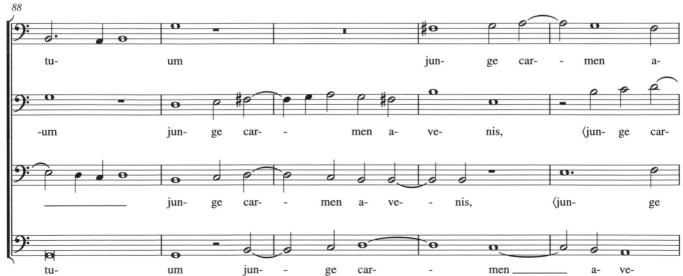

7. Dulces exuviae

Cantus
"Dul- ces ex- u- vi- ae, _____ dum fa-

Altus
"Dul- ces ex- u- vi- ae, dum fa-

Tenor 1
"Dul- ces ex- u- vi- ae, dum fa-

Tenor 2
"Dul- ces _____ ex- u- vi- ae, dum fa-

Bassus
"Dul- ces ex- u- vi- ae, dum fa-

-ta de- us- que si- ne- bat, ac- ci- - pi- te hanc a-

-ta de- us- que si- ne- bat, ac- ci- - pi- te hanc a-

-ta de- us- que si- ne- bat, ac- ci- - pi- te hanc a-

-ta de- us- que si- ne- bat, ac- ci- - pi- te hanc a-

-ta de- us- que si- ne- bat,

- ni- mam, ac- ci- - pi- te hanc a- - ni- mam me- que his

- ni- mam, ac- ci- - pi- te hanc a- - ni- mam me- que his

- ni- mam, ac- ci- - pi- te hanc a- - ni- mam me- que his

- ni- mam, ac- ci- - pi- te hanc a- - ni- mam me- que his

ac- ci- - pi- te hanc a- - ni- mam me- que his

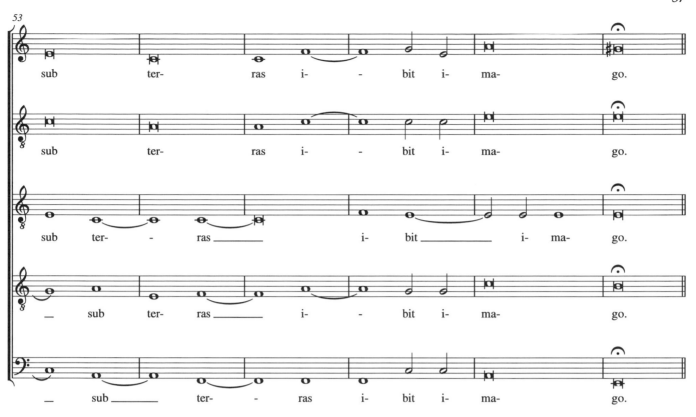

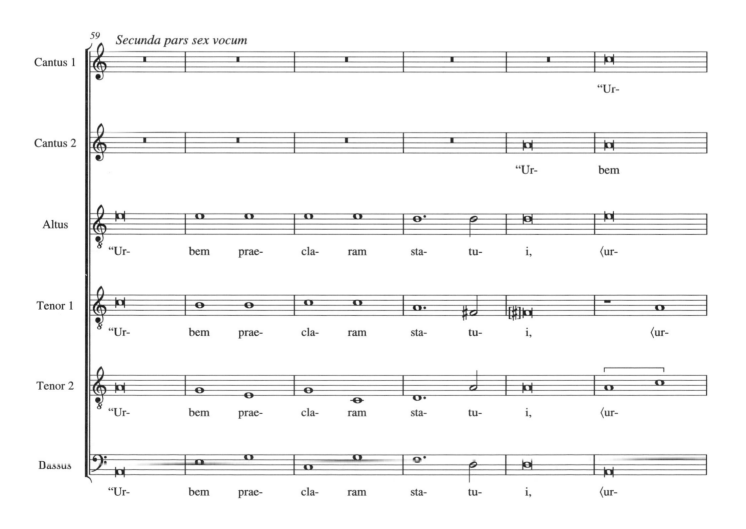

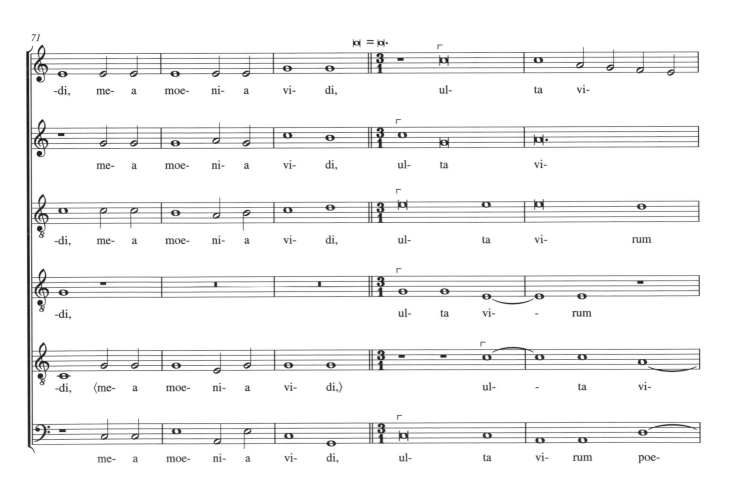

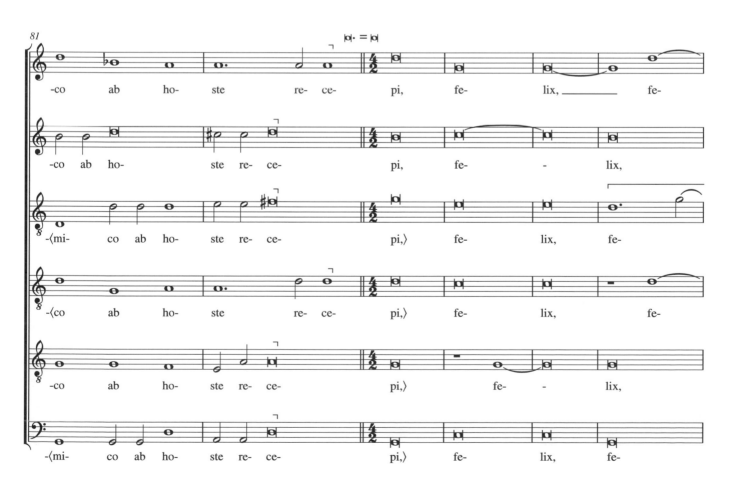

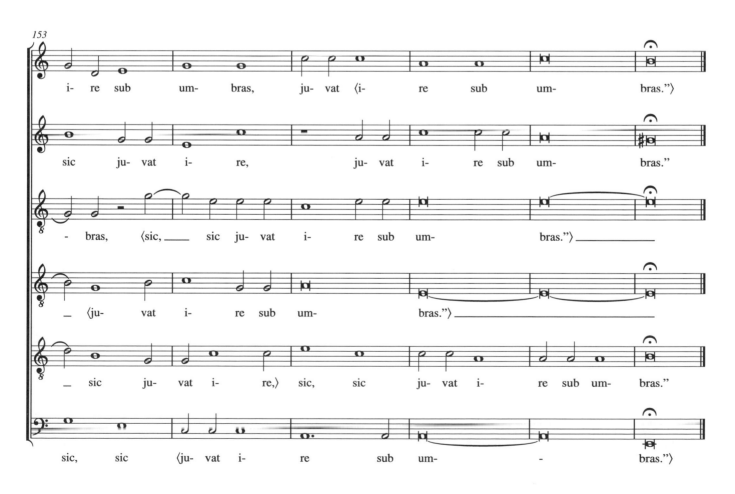

8. Alma Venus

48

50

9. Tityre, tu patulae

Cantus 1: Ti- ty- re, tu pa- tu- lae re- cu- bans sub te-

Cantus 2: Ti- ty- re, tu pa- tu- lae re- cu- bans sub te-

Altus: Ti- ty- re, tu pa- tu- lae re- cu- bans sub te-

Tenor: Ti- ty- re, tu pa- tu- lae re- cu- bans sub te-

Bassus 1: re- cu- bans sub te-

Bassus 2: re- cu- bans sub te-

-gmi- ne fa- gi, Syl- ve- strem te- nu- i Mu- - sam

-gmi- ne fa- gi, Syl- ve- strem te- - nu- i Mu- - sam

-gmi- ne fa- gi, Syl- ve- strem te- nu- i Mu- sam

-gmi- ne fa- gi, Syl- ve- strem, syl- ve- strem te- nu- i Mu- sam

-gmi- ne fa- gi, Syl- ve- strem te- nu- i Mu- sam

-gmi- ne fa- gi, Syl- ve- - strem te- nu- i Mu- sam

59

58 *Secunda pars*

65

62

10.Quia vidisti me, Thoma

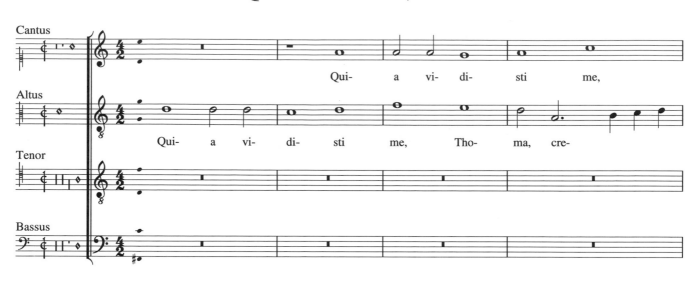

Cantus: Qui- a vi- di- sti me,

Altus: Qui- a vi- di- sti me, Tho- ma, cre-

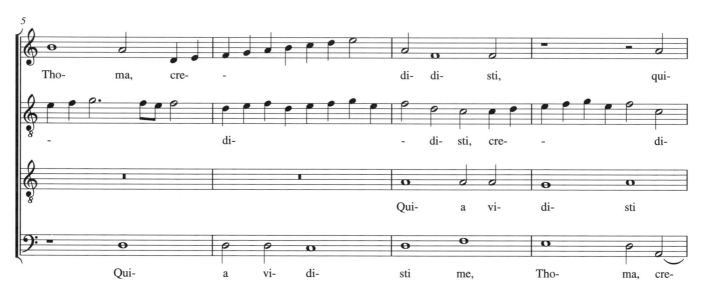

Cantus: Tho- ma, cre- - di- di- sti, qui

Altus: - di- - di- sti, cre- - di-

Tenor: Qui- a vi- di- sti

Bassus: Qui- a vi- di- sti me, Tho- ma, cre-

Cantus: -a vi- di- sti me, Tho- ma, (qui- a

Altus: -di- sti, cre- - di -

Tenor: me, Tho- ma, cre- di- -

Bassus: - di- di- sti, qui- a vi-

vi- di- sti me, Tho- - ma,⟩ cre- di- di-
-di- sti, cre- - di- di- - sti, cre- di- di- sti, ⟨cre-
-di- sti, qui- a vi- di- sti me, Tho-
-sti me, Tho- ma, ⟨qui- a vi- di- sti me, Tho- ma,⟩

-sti: be- a- ti qui non vi- de- runt, be- a-
- di- di- sti:⟩ _____ be- a- ti qui non vi- de- runt, ⟨be-
-ma, _____ cre- di- di- - sti: be- a- ti qui
cre- di- di- - sti:

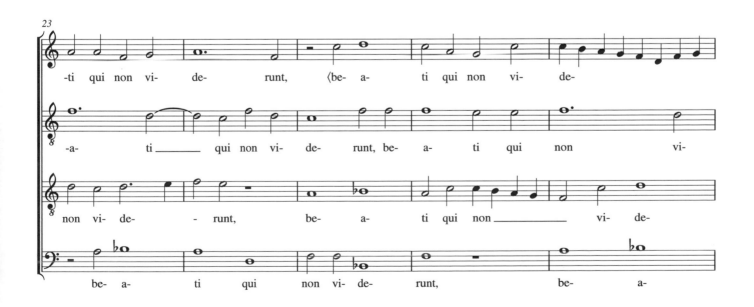

-ti qui non vi- de- runt, ⟨be- a- ti qui non vi- de-
-a- ti _____ qui non vi- de- runt, be- a- ti qui non vi-
non vi- de- - runt, be- a- ti qui non _____ vi- de-
be- a- ti qui non vi- de- runt, be- a-

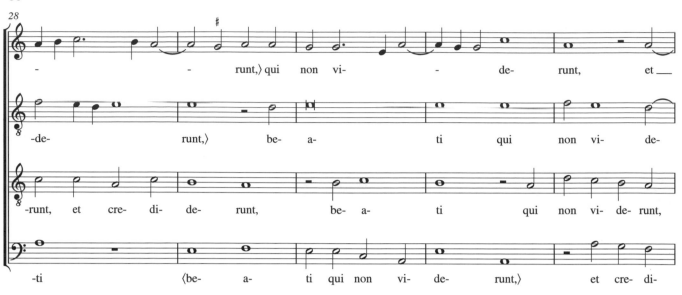

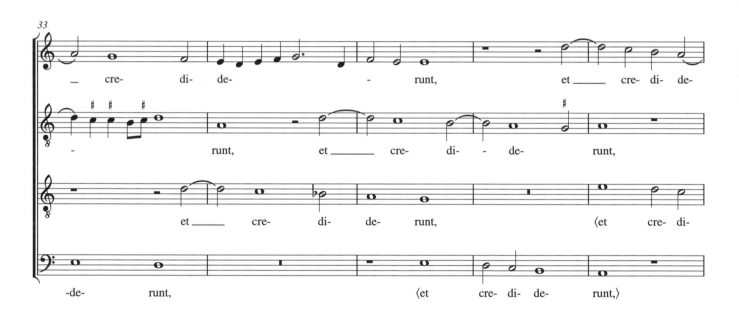

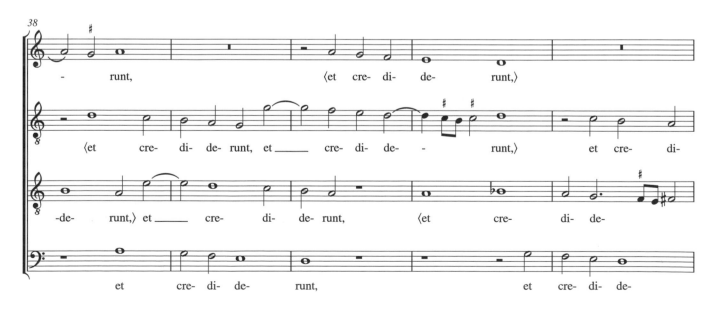

11. Scio enim quod redemptor meus vivit

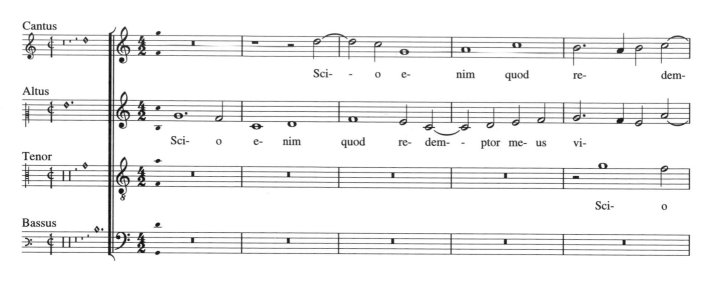

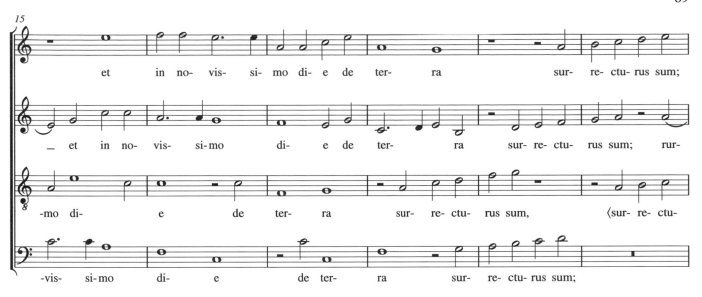

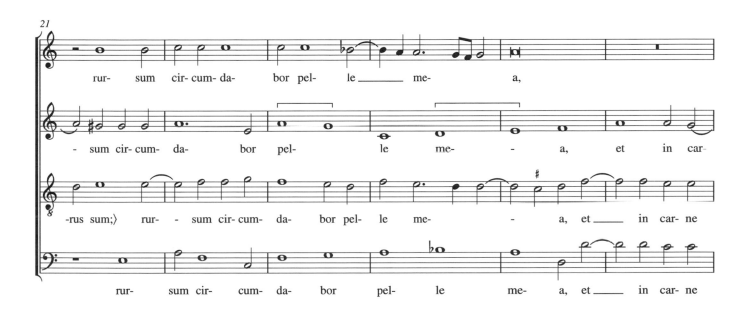

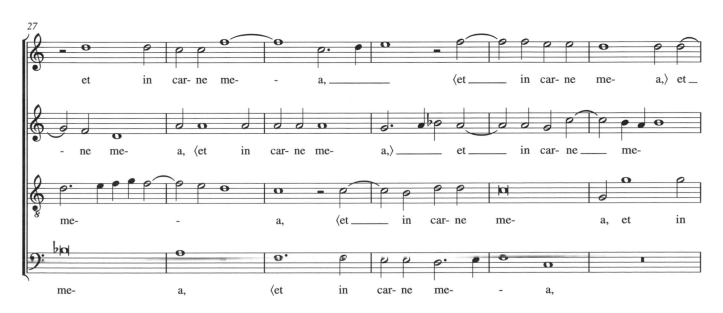

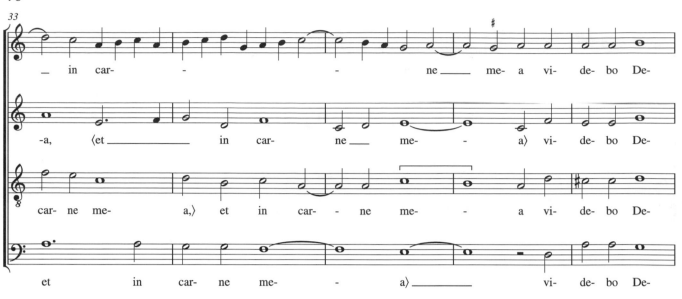

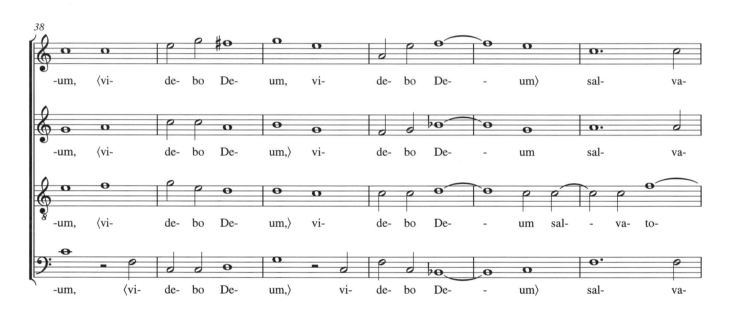

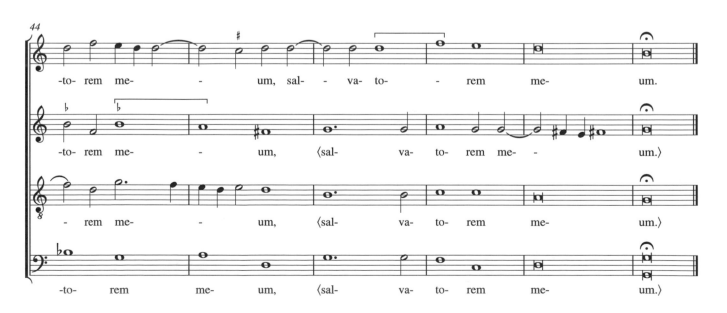

12. Fertur in conviviis

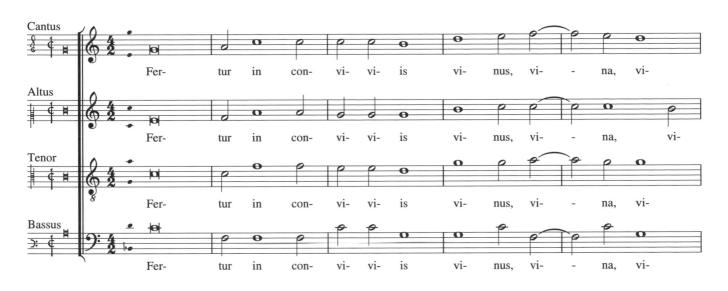

Cantus / Altus / Tenor / Bassus

Fer- tur in con- vi- vi- is vi- nus, vi- na, vi-

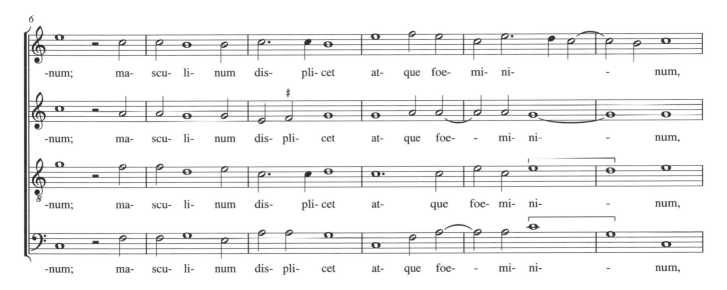

-num; ma- scu- li- num dis- pli- cet at- que foe- mi- ni- num,

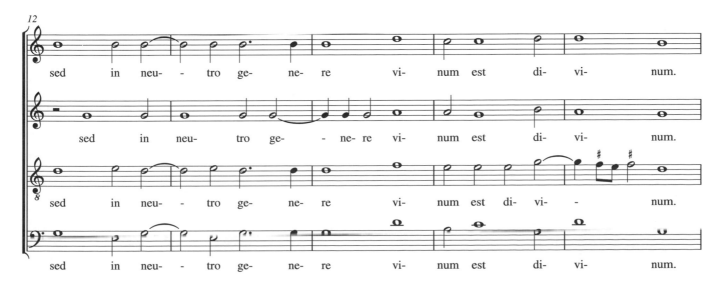

sed in neu- tro ge- ne- re vi- num est di- vi- num.

72

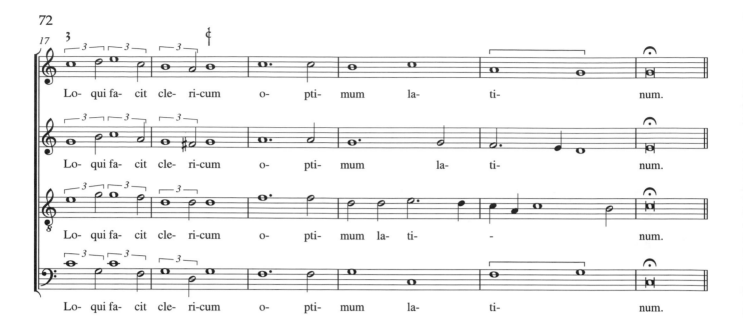

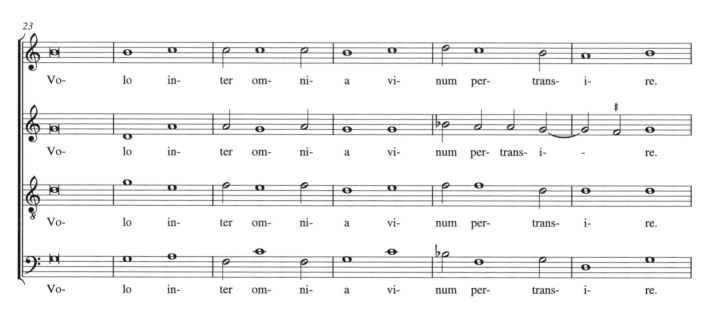

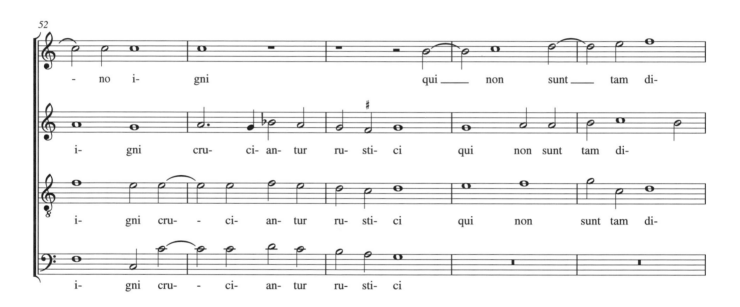

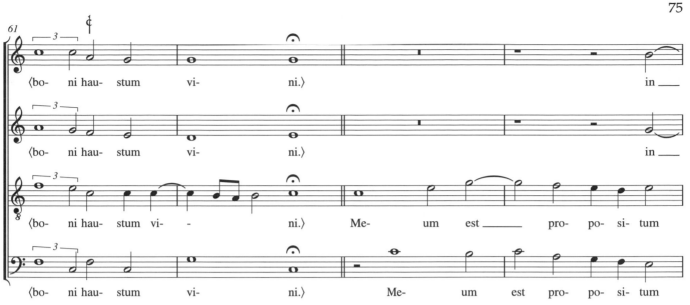

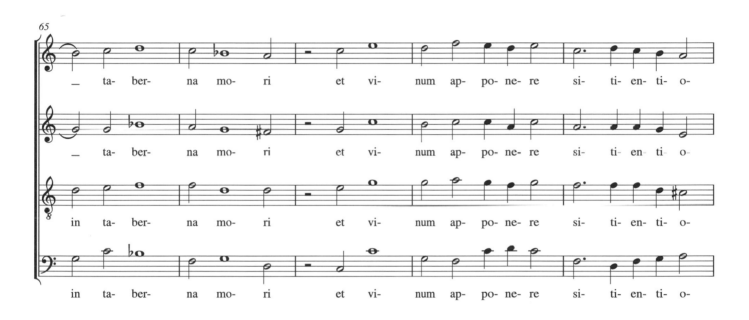

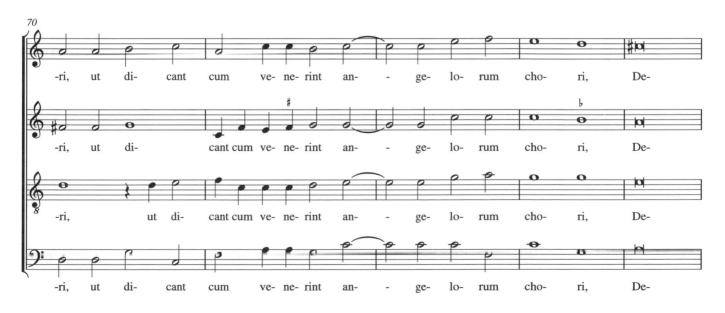

-us   sit   pro- pi- ti- us   hu-   ic   po-   ta- to-   ri.

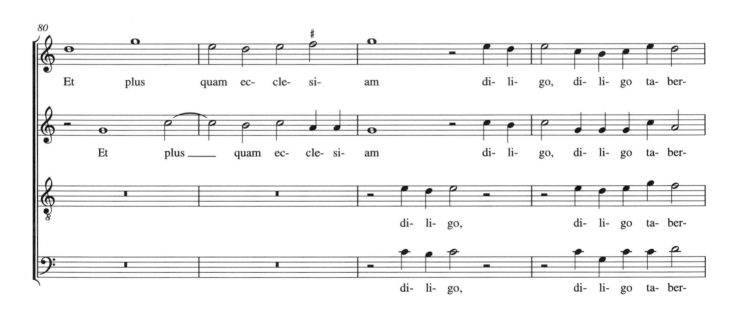

Et   plus   quam ec- cle- si- am   di- li- go, di- li- go ta- ber-

Et   plus ___ quam ec- cle- si- am   di- li- go, di- li- go ta- ber-

di- li- go,   di- li- go ta- ber-

di- li- go,   di- li- go ta- ber-

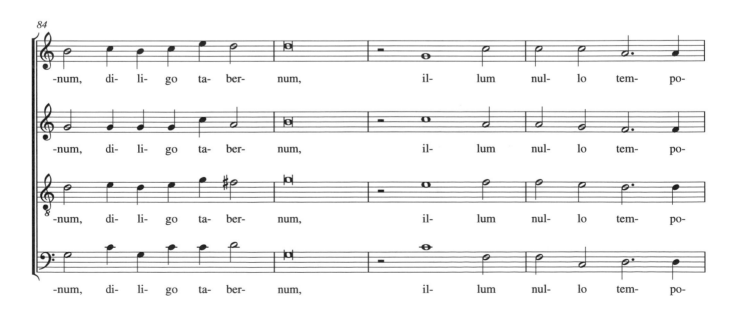

-num, di- li- go ta- ber- num,   il- lum nul- lo tem- po-

-num, di- li- go ta- ber- num,   il- lum nul- lo tem- po-

-num, di- li- go ta- ber- num,   il- lum nul- lo tem- po-

-num, di- li- go ta- ber- num,   il- lum nul- lo tem- po-

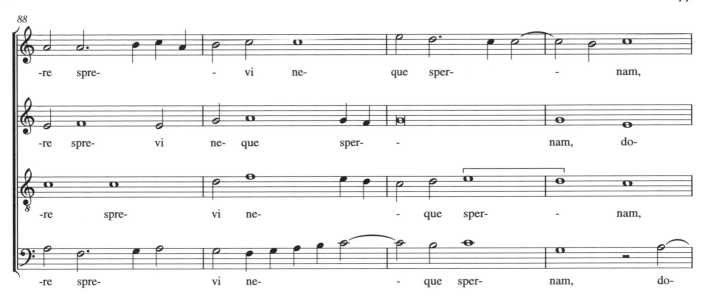

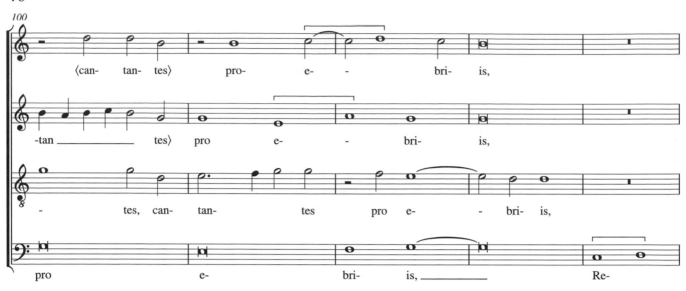

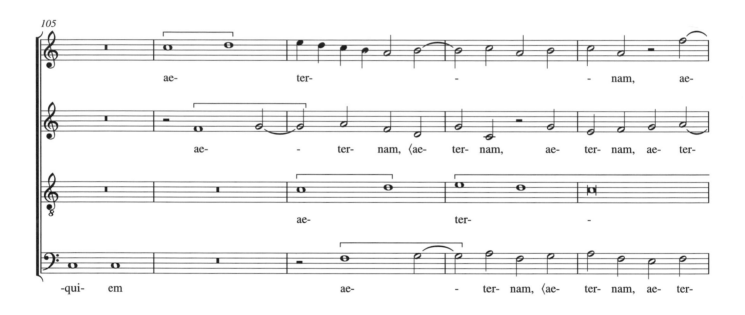

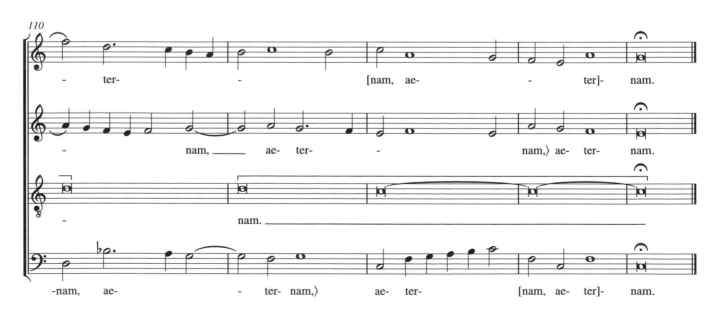

13. Quid prodest stulto

14. Pater, peccavi

15. Deus qui bonum vinum creasti

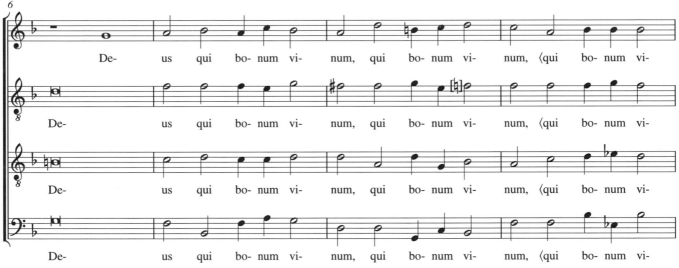

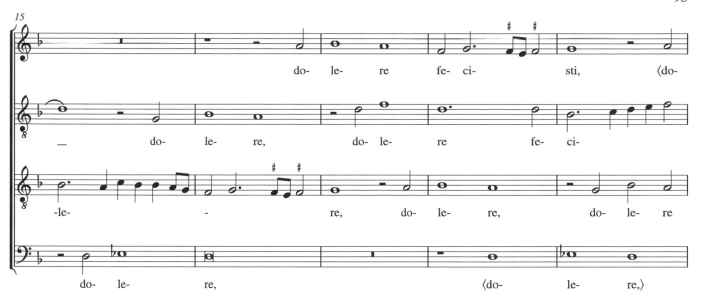

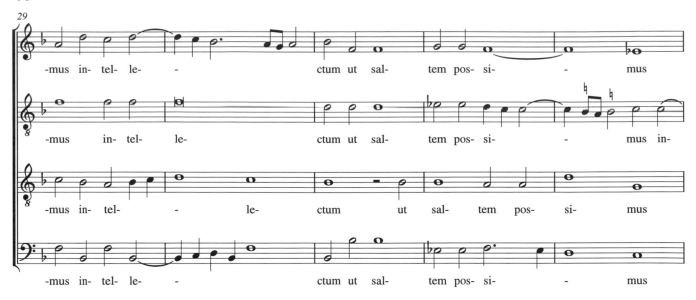

-mus in- tel- le - - ctum ut sal- tem pos- si - - mus

-mus in- tel- le- - ctum ut sal- tem pos- si - - mus in-

-mus in- tel- - le- ctum ut sal- tem pos- si- mus

-mus in- tel- le- - ctum ut sal- tem pos- si - - mus

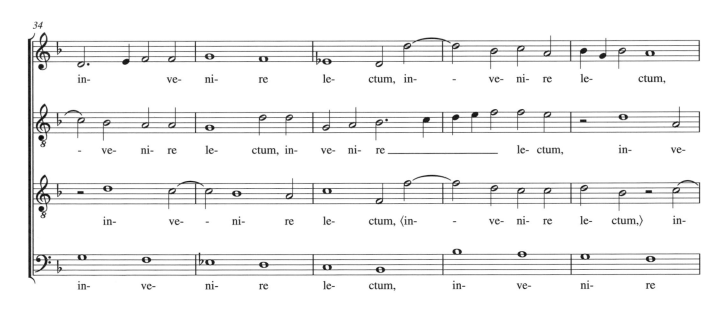

in- ve- ni- re le- ctum, in - ve- ni- re le- ctum,

- ve- ni- re le- ctum, in- ve- ni- re _____ le- ctum, in- ve-

in- ve - ni- re le- ctum, ⟨in - ve- ni- re le- ctum,⟩ in-

in- ve- ni- re le- ctum, in- ve- ni- re

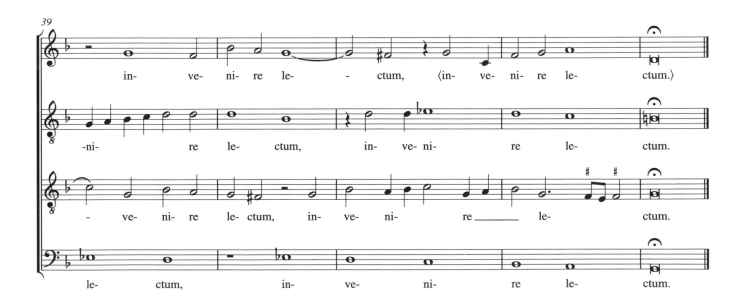

in- ve- ni- re le- - ctum, ⟨in- ve- ni- re le- ctum.⟩

-ni- re le- ctum, in- ve- ni- re le- ctum.

- ve- ni- re le- ctum, in- ve- ni- re _____ le- ctum.

le- ctum, in- ve- ni- re le- ctum.

16. Forte soporifera

17. Quis est homo qui timet Dominum?

18. Ubi est Abel

19. Quem dicunt homines

20. Jesu, nostra redemptio

126

21. S, U, su, P, E, R, per

22. Audi, benigne conditor

23. Domine, quando veneris (2)

24. Tribulationem et dolorem inveni

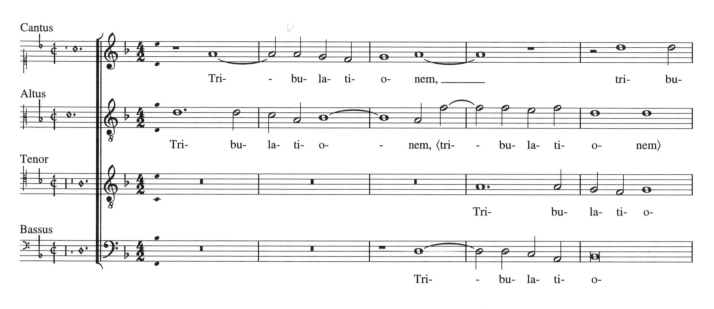

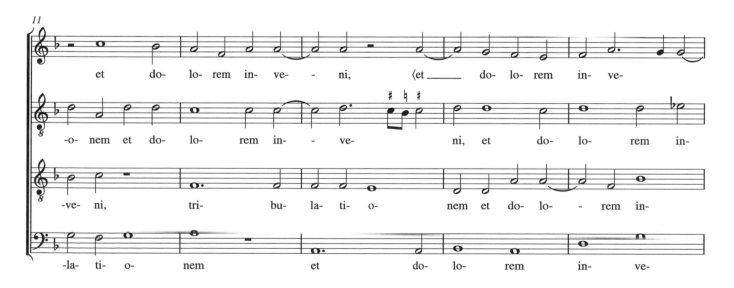

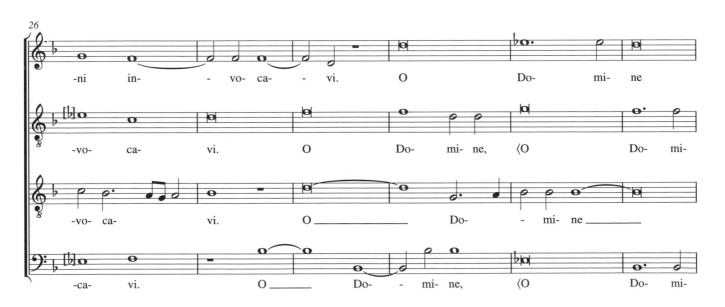

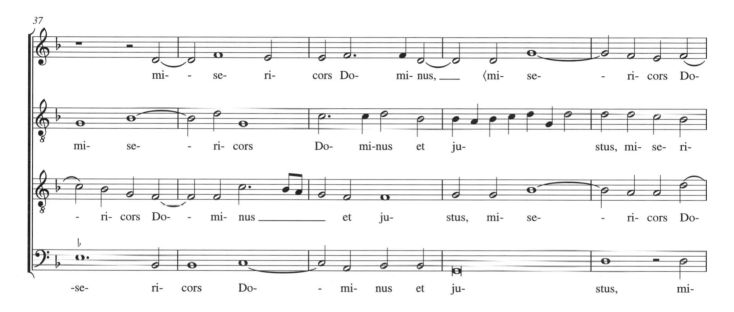

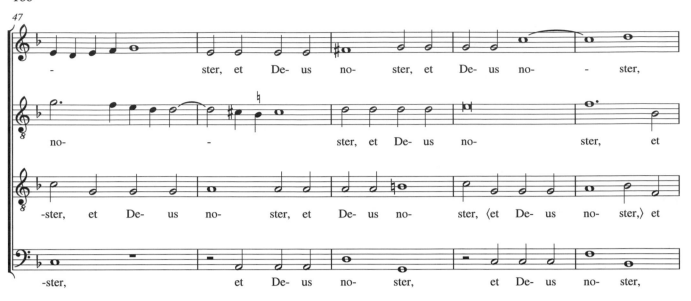

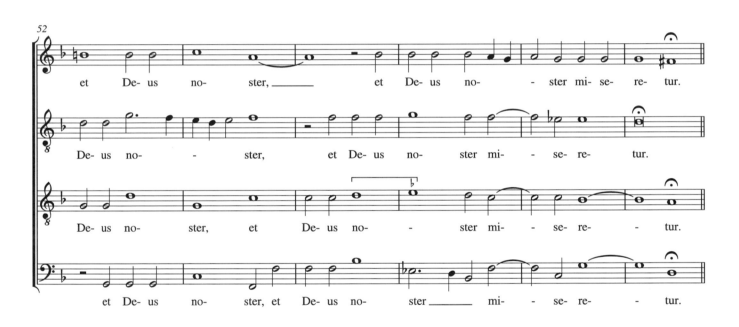

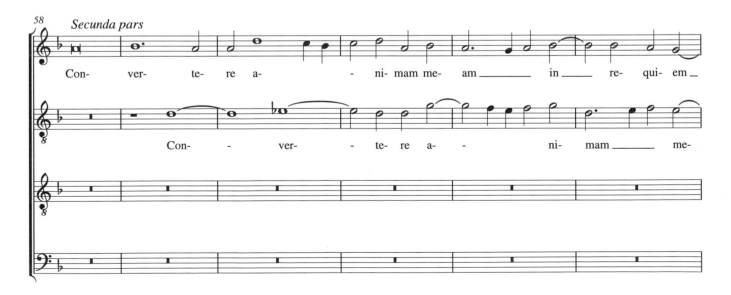

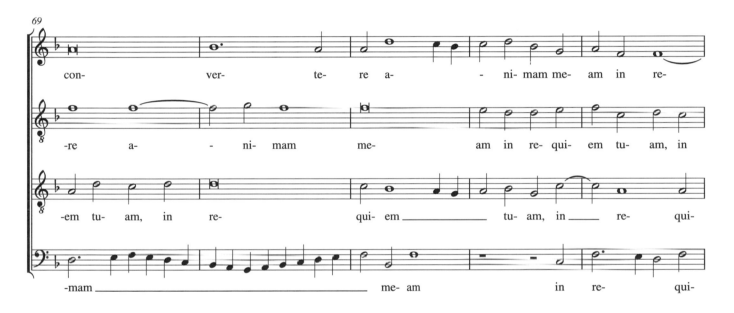

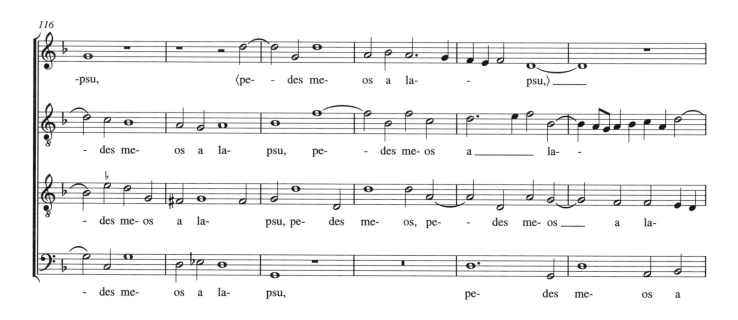

25. Laetentur caeli

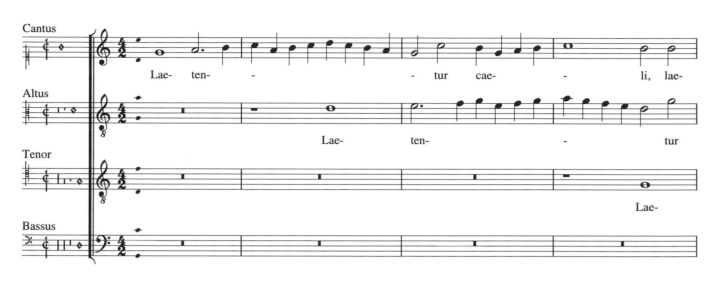

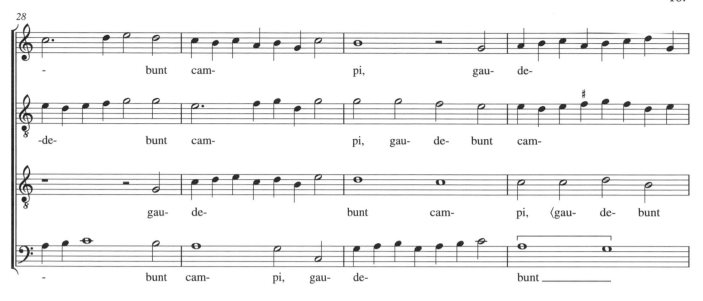

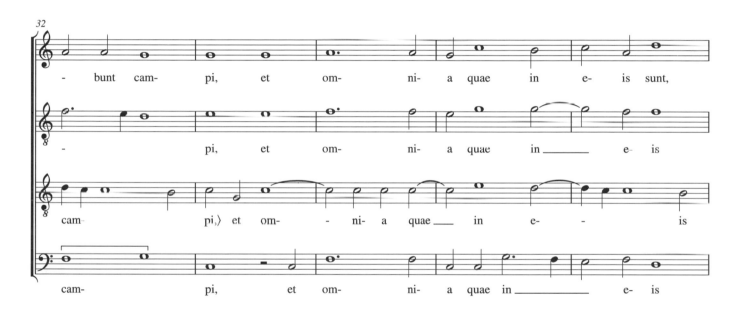

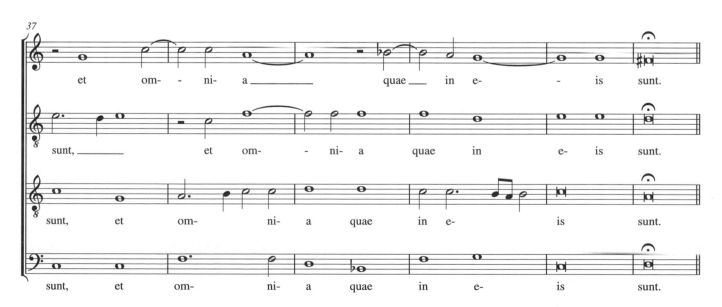

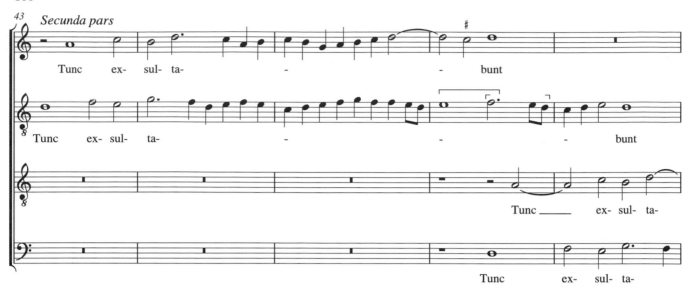

Secunda pars

Tunc ex- sul- ta- - - bunt

Tunc ex- sul- ta- - - - bunt

Tunc _____ ex- sul- ta-

Tunc ex- sul- ta-

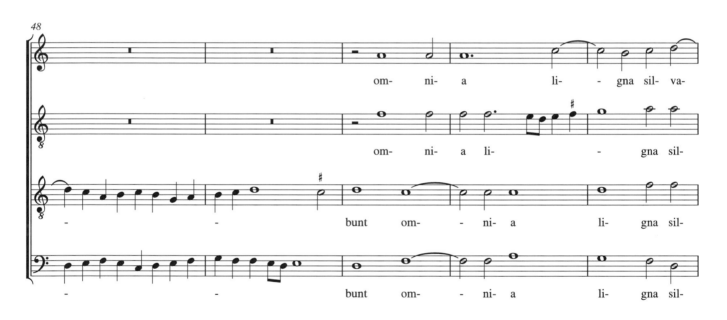

om- ni- a li- gna sil- va

om- ni- a li- - gna sil-

- - bunt om- - ni- a li- gna sil-

- - bunt om- - ni- a li- gna sil-

- rum a fa- ci- e Do- - mi-

-va- rum a fa- ci- e Do- mi- ni, _____ qui-

-va- rum a fa- ci- e Do- mi- ni, a fa- ci- e Do-

-va- rum a fa- ci- e Do- - mi- ni, qui-

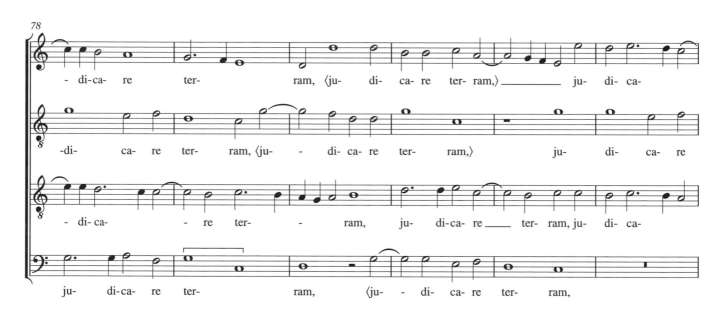

26. Fratres, sobrii estote

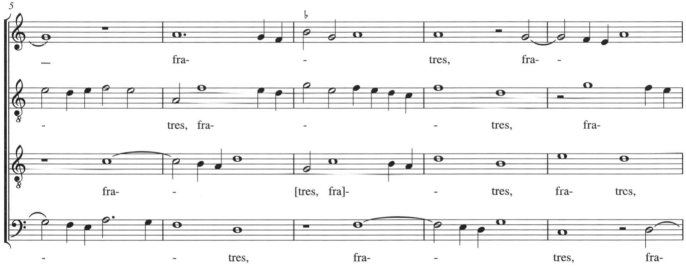

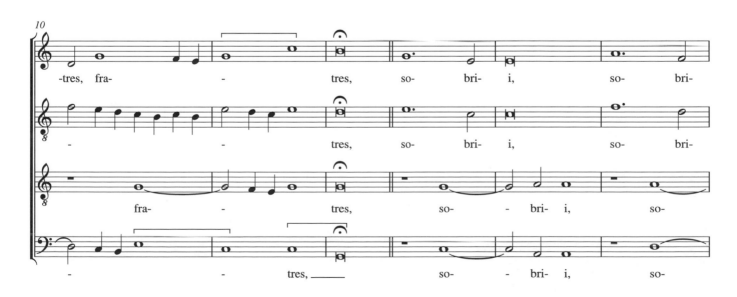

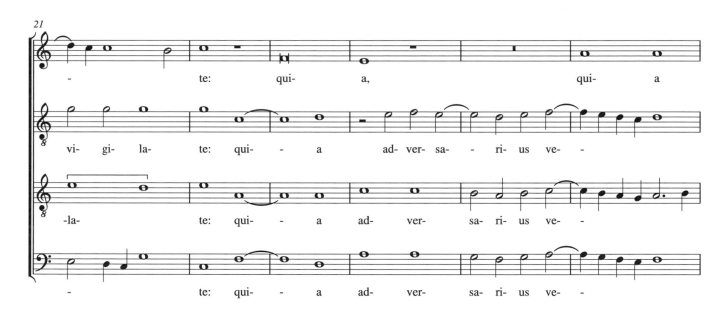

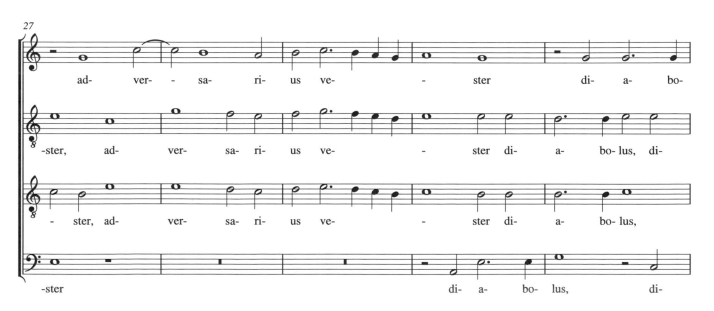

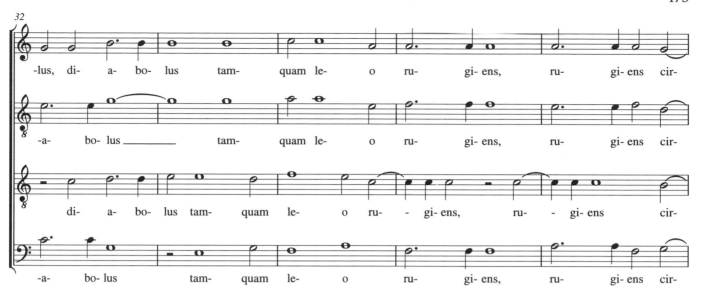

Critical Report

Sources

Because of the large number of sources used in the preparation of this volume, the individual sources will not be described physically in as much detail as in other volumes of *CM*. However, the contents of many of the sources are given so that the position of Lasso's motets in those sources may be seen.

The following sources were used in preparing this edition.

RISM 1555b: LE QVATOIRSIESME | Liure a quatre parties contenant, | *DIXHUYCT CHANSONS ITA-* | *liennes,* *Six chansons francoises, & Six Motetz. faictz* | *(a la Nouuelle composition d'aucuns d'Italie) par* | *Rolando di Lassus Nou-* *uellement Impri-* | *me en Anuers par Tylman Susato* | *Imprimeur de Musicque.* | SVPERIVS. [CONTRATENOR., TENOR., BASSVS.] | *AVECQ GRACE ET PRIVI-* | *lege de* *la Maieste Imperiale. pour quatre* | *ans. Lan M. D. LV Soub-* | *signe de Lange.*

There are four partbooks: superius, contratenor, tenor, and bassus. I used the facsimile edition of the sole surviving copy held by the Musikabteilung der Bayerische Staatsbibliothek, Munich (Brussells: Éditions Culture et Civilisation, 1972). The source is highly accurate with no significant errors to report. The contents follow; all are by Lasso except the last motet.

Madrigals
1–6. Del freddo Rheno (sestina)
  7. Per pianto la mia carne
  8. Queste non son più lagrime
  9. Se ben l'empia mia sorte
10. Occhi piangete accompagnate il core
11. Vatene lieta homai coppia d'amici
12. Perch'io veggio

Villanesche
13. Madonna mia, pietà chiam'et aita
14. Tu sai, madonna mia, ch'io t'amo et voglio
15. 'No giorno t'haggio havere intra 'ste mane
16. La cortesia voi donne predicate
17. Tu, traditora, m'hai puost'a 'sto core
18. 'Sto core mio se fosse di diamante

Chansons
19. Las voulez-vous
20. En espoir vis et crainte
21. Avec vous mon amour finira
22. Je l'ayme bien
23. Trop endurer sans avoir
24. Vray dieu disoit une fillette

Motets
25. Audi dulcis amica mea
26. Peccantem me quotidie
27. Inclina Domine aurem tuam
28. Domine, quando veneris
29. Alma Nemes
30. Calami sonum ferentes, *Cipriano de Rore*

Mu 20: Munich, Bayerische Staatsbibliothek, Mus. Ms. 20 (microfilm). This manuscript from the Bavarian *Hofkapelle* was copied ca. 1560 by one of the court copyists. A full description and list of contents may be found in *KBM5/1*, 91–92. Most of the manuscript was copied from Lasso's 1556 motet book (see *CM 1*), but no. 1, fols. 1v–15r, is "Pater, peccavi," no. 14 in this volume, and no. 20, fols. 190v–203r, is "Dulces exuviae," no. 7 in this volume. Mu 20 predates the earliest printed sources for both motets, by about four and ten years respectively. Mu 20 is used as a concurrent source for "Pater, peccavi," but because of the greater time difference between sources, "Dulces exuviae" is placed in *CM 17* according to the date of Mu 20. Mu 20 is not always careful in underlay and indication of text repetitions, as pointed out in *CM 1* and *CM 5*, and the printed sources for both motets have been given more weight in this regard.

RISM 1560b: TIERS LIVRE DES | CHANSONS A QVA-TRE | CINCQ ET SIX PARTIES NOVELLEMENT | composez par Orlando di Laissus [*sic*] Conuenables tant | aux instrumentez comme à la Voix. | SVPERIVS [CONTRA-TENOR, TENOR, BASSVS, QVINTA PARS]. | Imprime à Louain par Pierre Phalese Libraire Iure. Lan. M.D. LX. | Avecq Grace & priuilege.

There are five partbooks: superius, contratenor, tenor, bassus, and quinta pars. I used a microfilm of the sole surviving complete copy held by the Murhard'sche

Bibliothek der Stadt und Landesbibliothek, Kassel, 4° Mus. 62b^c. The contents are mostly first editions except for the chansons reprinted from RISM 1555b, and are listed below. The two motets, "Alma Venus" and "Tityre, tu patulae," are nos. 8 and 9 in this volume. The faulty text of the two motets, especially "Tityre, tu patulae," has been corrected from other sources. In addition, RISM 1560b includes only the *prima pars* of "Tityre, tu patulae." I have supplied the *secunda pars* from a later source.

1. Las voulez-vous
2. En espoir vis et crainte
3. Avec vous mon amour finira
4. Je l'ayme bien
5. Trop endurer sans avoir
6. Vray dieu disoit une fillette
7. Hélas quel jour
8. Ung doulx nenny
9. In dubbio di mio stato
10. Est il possible à moy
11. Alma Venus (2 partes)
12. Elle s'en va de moy
13. Le rossignol plaisant
14. Veux-tu ton mal
15. Sur tout regretz
16. Las me fault-il
17. Mon couer se recommande
18. Vous qui aymez les dames
19. Ardent amour souvent
20. J'attends le tems
21. Susanne un jour
22. Un triste coeur rempli
23. Tityre, tu patulae (*prima pars* only)

RISM 1563³: ALTUS | LIBER PRIMVS MVSARVM | CVM QVATTVOR VOCIBVS | SACRARVM CANTIONVM QVE VVLGO MOTETTA VOCANTVR | AB ORLANDO DI LASSVS, | CIPRIANO RORE, ET ALIIS ECCLESIAS-TICIS AVTHORIBVS | compositarum, ab Antonio Barrè collectarum & in lucem | nunc primum editarum. | CVM PRIVILEGIO. | QVATVOR [design] VOCVM |VENETIIS apud Franciscum Rampazetum | 1563.

There are four partbooks: cantus, altus, tenor, and bassus. I used a microfilm copy of the only surviving complete set of part books at the Civico Museo Bibliografico Musicale, Bologna. The two Lasso first editions, "Quia vidisti me, Thoma," and "Scio enim quod redemptor meus vivit," are nos. 10 and 11 in this volume. Their texts are nearly error free, especially when compared to reprints in RISM 1566f and 1568b. The contents of RISM 1563³ are listed as they appear in the source's index.

1. Orlando Lassus. Quia vidisti me Thoma
2. Gio. Pe. Loysius Prenestinus. O quam suavis
3. Orlandus Lassus. Alma nemes
4. Clemens non Papa. Amici mei; 2. p. Ego autem
5. Cipriano Rore. Beati omnes qui timent; 2. p. Ecce sic

6. Orlandus Lassus. Inclina Dne aurem tuam
7. Orlandus Lassus. Scio enim quod redemptor meus
8. Maillart. Domine Jesu Christe; 2. p. Nam sponsum
9. Lerma. Beata es virgo Maria
10. Orlandus Lassus. Peccantem me quotidie
11. Gio. Petrus loysius Prenestinus. Nativitas tua dei genitrix
12. Lerma. Ave virginum gemma
13. Adrian Valent. Inclina domine aurem tuam; 2. p. Tu es enim auditor meus
14. Josquin Baston. Factum est cor meum
15. Cipriano Rore. O crux benedicta (cum paribus vocibus)
16. Paolo Animuccia. Tribularer si nescirem; 2. p. Secundem multitudinem
17. Cipriano Rore. Caro mea vera est cibus; 2. p. Hic est panis
18. Adrian Valent. O sacrum convivium
19. Domine quando veneris [Lasso]
20. Audi dulcis amica [Lasso]
21. Annibale Zoilo. Petite & accipietis
22. Lupi. Surge propera amica; 2. p. Surge

RISM 1564d: QVATRIESME LIVRE DES | CHANSONS A QVATRE | ET CINCQ PARTIES NOVVELLEMENT | composées par Orlando di Lassus, conuenables tant aux | Instruments comme a la Voix. Louvain: Pierre Phalèse, 1564.

A complete description and full list of contents may be found in Henri Vanhulst, *Catalogue des éditions de musique publiées à Louvain par Pierre Phalèse et ses fils 1545–1578* (Brussels: Académie Royale de Belgique, Classe des beaux-arts, 1990). I used the only surviving complete copy held at the Bayerische Staatsbibliothek, Munich. RISM 1564d contains three motets that are first editions (nos. 12, 13, and 14 in this volume): no. 9, "Fertur in conviviis," no. 21, "Quid prodest stulto," and no. 23, "Pater, peccavi." The text of all three motets in RISM 1564d is faulty and requires extensive emendation from other sources.

RISM 1565a: MODVLORVM | ORLANDI DE LASSVS. | quaternis, quinis, sênis, septenis, octonis | & denis vocibus modulatorum | SECVNDVM VOLVMEN. | LVTETIÆ PARISIORVM. | Apud Adrianum le Roy, & Robertum Ballard, | Regis Typographos. sub signo | montis Parnassi. | 1565 | Cum priuilegio Regis ad decennium. | CONTRATENOR. [TENOR., BASSVS., QVINTA PARS].

There are five partbooks: superius, contratenor, tenor, bassus, and quinta pars. No copy of the superius book is known to survive. I used microfilm copies of the contratenor, tenor, and bassus from the Bibliothèque Sainte-Geneviève, Paris, and the quinta pars from the Bayerische Staatsbibliothek, Munich. For a full description and list of contents of this source see *CM 4*. It was used in this volume to correct the text of no. 14, "Pater, peccavi."

RISM 1565c: CANTVS [ALTVS, TENOR, BASSVS, QVINTVS, SEXTVS] | ORLANDI LASSI CHORI BAVARIAE | DVCIS MAGISTRI. | QVINQVE ET SEX VOCIBVS PERORNATAE, | Sacræ cantiones nunc primum omni diligentia in lucem editæ, | à Iulio Bonagiunta Musico Ecclesiæ divi Marci | Venetiarum. | liber secundus. | CVM GRATIA ET PRIVILEGIO. | Venetiis, apud Hieronymum Scottum. | M D L X V.

For a full description and list of contents of this source see *CM 5*. I used a microfilm copy of the only surviving complete set of partbooks, held by the Civico Museo Bibliografico Musicale, Bologna. It was used in this volume to correct the text of no. 13, "Quid prodest stulto."

RISM 1565f: *TENOR.* | DIXHVICTIEME LIVRE. | DE CHANSONS A QVATRE | & à cinq parties par Orlande de lassus, | Imprimé en quatre volumes. | A PARIS. | Par Adrian le Roy, & Robert Ballard, Imprimeurs | du Roy. | *1565.* | Auec priuilege de sa maiesté | Pour dix ans.

A full description of this source may be found in François Lesure and Geneviève Thibault, *Bibliographie des éditions d'Adrian Le Roy et Robert Ballard (1551–1598)* (Paris: Heugel, 1955), 121, no. 109. I used a microfilm copy of the contratenor, tenor, and bassus partbooks, which are all that survive, from the Bibliothèque Nationale, Paris. This is the earliest known source for no. 15 in this volume, "Deus qui bonum vinum creasti." For the superius partbook see RISM 1573i below.

RISM 1566c: CANTVS [ALTVS, TENOR, BASSVS, QVINTVS] | ORLANDI LASSI | SACRAE CANTIONES (VVLGO MOTECTA | APPELLATAE) QVINQVE, ET SEX VOCVM, | Tum uiua uoce tum omnis generis Instrumentis cantatu commodissimæ. | LIBER SECVNDVS | Venetijs Appud | Antonium Gardanum. | 1566.

For a full description and list of contents of this source see *CM 5*. I used a microfilm copy of the complete set of partbooks held by the Bayerische Staatsbibliothek, Munich. It was used in this volume to correct the text of no. 13, "Quid prodest stulto."

RISM 1566f: SACRAE LECTIONES NOVEM | EX PROPHETA IOB, QVATVOR VOCVM, IN | OFFICIIS DEFVNCTORVM CANTARI SOLITÆ. | AVTORE ORLANDO LASSO. | *His adiecta sunt Muteta quædam harmonia pari* | *eodem Autore.* | *SVPERIVS.* | LOVANII. | Apud Petrum Phalesium Bibliopol. Iurat. Anno. M.D.LXVI. | Cum gratia & priuilegio.

I used a microfilm copy of the superius, contratenor, and bassus partbooks, which are all that survive, held by the Österreichisches Nationalbibliothek, Vienna. It contains four motets reprinted from RISM 1555b, nos. 1–4 in this volume, and "Quia vidisti me, Thoma," no. 10 in this volume. Two variants in the latter motet are reported below.

RISM 1566¹⁷: CANTO | DI CIPRIANO DE RORE | IL QVINTO LIBRO DI MADRIGALI | A CINQUE VOCI INSIEME ALCVNI DE DIVERSI | Autori Nouamente per Antonio Gardano stampato & dato in Luce. | A CINQVE VOCI | CON GRATIA ET PRIVILLEGGIO. | In Venetia Appresso | di Antonio Gardano. | 1566.

I used a microfilm copy of the only surviving complete set of partbooks (canto, alto, tenore, basso, quinto), held by the British Library, London. It contains as no. 15 "Forte soporifera," no. 16 in this volume, for which it is the earliest known source. As usual, Gardano gives an accurate text; only a few small emendations of underlay were necessary.

RISM 1567³: ALTO | PRIMO LIBRO DE GLI ETERNI | MOTTETTI DI ORLANDO LASSO | CIPRIANO RORE ET D'ALTRI ECCEL. | MVSICI, A CINQVE ET SEI VOCI, | Di nouo posti in luce per Giulio Bonagionta da San Genesi | Musico della Illustriss. Signoria di Venetia in S. Marco | & con ogni diligentia corretti. | [design] | IN VINEGIA M D LXVII. | APPRESSO GIROLAMO SCOTTO.

Only the alto partbook of this source survives, in the Conservatorio di Musica Santa Cecilia, Rome. It includes four Lasso motets, nos. 17–20 in this volume, for all of which it is the earliest known source. The next earliest source for all four motets is RISM 1568a and 1568b, which were used as the source for this edition. The contents of RISM 1567³ are as follows:

1. Quis es homo, Lasso
2. Ubi est Abel, Lasso
3. Quem dicunt homines, Lasso
4. Ad te levavi oculos meos (3 partes), Rore
5. Parcius Estenses, G. Zarlino
6. Ave Regina caelorum, Michael de Cornis
7. Ave Regina caelorum, Innocentio Alberti
8. Sub tuum praesidium, Portinaro
9. Super omnia lingua, Leandro Mira
10. Inclina Domine aurem tuam (2 partes), Stefano Rosetto
11. Da pacem Domine, Giacomo Migre
12. Descendit de caelis, Londarito
13. Jesu, nostra redemptio (4 partes), Lasso
14. Vidi coniunctos viros, Caesare Schieti
15. Peccantem me quotidie, Andrea Gabrieli

RISM 1567¹³: BASSO | SECONDO LIBRO DELLE FIAMME | MADRIGALI A CINQUE ET SEI VOCI | DE DIVERSI ECCELENTISSIMI MVSICI | Di nouo posto in luce per Giulio Bonagionta da San Genesi | Musico della Illustriss. Signoria in Venetia in S. Marco | & con ogni diligentia corretti. | IN VINEGIA M D LXVII. | APPRESSO GIROLAMO SCOTTO

This is the earliest source for no. 21 in the present volume, "S, U, su, P, E, R, per." Only four of its five partbooks survive: canto in Civico Museo Bibliografico Musicale,

Bologna; alto in Bibliothèque Royale, Brussels; quinto in Conservatorio di Musica Santa Cecilia, Rome; basso in British Library, London. I used microfilm of them and of the complete set of partbooks for the reprint, RISM 1570[14], held by the Bayerische Staatsbibliothek, Munich. The contents of 1567[13] are as follows:

1. Claudio Correggio. Da bei raggi; 2.p. Quindi giusto desio
2. Alessandro Striggio. Di questa biond' & vaga
3. Alessandro Striggio. L pastorella
4. Anibal Padouano. Voi che'ri vista; 2.p. Ivi è la spenta
5. Vetto. Raimondo. Solinga Tortorella; 2.p. Ma io lasso
6. Vetto. Raimondo. Occhi miei dolci; 2.p. Deh Deh per-ch'oscura e trista
7. Pietro Taglia. Se di penne
8. D'Incerto. Poi ch'il mio largo pianto
9. Michel de Cornis. Oime ch'in tutt'io
10. Lorenzo Benvenuti. Giunto Adrian; 2.p. Di aqua i grandi del mondo
11. Cesare Schieti. Non mi parto da voi
12. Orlando Lasso. S. U. su P. E. R. per; 2.p. I. L. il L. I. C.
13. Giovan Ferretti. Questa sera gentil
14. Alessandro Striggio. Dolce ritorn' Amor
15. Alessandro Striggio. Questi ch'inditio
16. Cesare Schieti. Era nubil il ciel

RISM1568a: SELECTISSIMÆ CANTI- | ONES, QVAS VVLGO MOTETAS VOCANT, PARTIM OM- | NINO NOVAE, PARTIM NVSQVAM IN GERMANIA EXCVSAE, | *Sex & pluribus uocibus compositæ per excellen-* | *tißimum Musicum,* | Orlandum di Lassus. | DISCANTVS [ALTVS, TENOR, BASSVS, QVINTA VOX, SEXTA VOX] | NORIBERGÆ, | APVD THEODORICVM GER-LATZENVM, IN | Officina Ioannis Montani piæ memo-riæ. | M. D. LXVIII.

RISM 1568b: SELECTISSIMÆ | CANTIONES, QVAS | VVLGO MOTETAS VOCANT, PARTIM OMNINO | NOVAE, PARTIM NVSQVAM IN GERMANIA EXCVSAE, | QVINQVE ET QVATVOR VOCIBVS COM-POSITAE PER | EXCELLENTISSIMVM MVSICVM, | Orlandum di Lassus. | DISCANTVS [ALTVS, TENOR, BASSVS, VAGANS] | NORIBERGÆ, | Apud Theodori-cum Gerlatzenum, in Officina Ioannis | Montani piæ memoriæ. | M. D. LXVIII.

For a full description and list of contents of these sources see *CM 6*. They have been used in this volume to supply texts for motets printed in some earlier sources that do not survive complete and to help correct the texts of other motets. In addition, RISM 1568a is the earliest known source for the second part of no. 9, "Tityre, tu patulae."

RISM 1568[2]: TENOR | NOVI THESAVRI | MUSICI | LIBER PRIMUS | QVO SELECTISSIMAE | Planeque novae, nec vnquam in luce aeditae | cantiones sacrae (quas vulgo moteta vo- | cant) continentur octo, septem, sex, quinque | ac quatuor vocum, a praestantissimis ac | huius aetatis, precipuis Symphoniacis | compositae, quae

in sacra Ecclesia catho- | lica, summis solemnibusque fes-tiuitatibus, | canuntur, ad omnis generis instrumenta | musica, accomodatae: Petri Ioannelli | Bergomensis de Gandino, summo | studio ac labore collectae, eiusque | expensis impressae. | Venetijs Apud Antonium Gar-danum. 1568 | CUM GRAT: ET PRIVIL: | Sac: Ro: Cae: Ma: Et Ill: Senatus Venet:

RISM 1568[4]: TENOR | NOVI ATQVE | CATHOLICI THE- | SAURI MUSICI. | LIBER TERTIUS | QVO SELECTISSI-MAE | Planeque novæ, nec vnquam in lucem | editæ can-tiones sacræ, quas vulgo moteta | vocant, octo, septem, sex, quinque, quatuor | vocum compositæ à praestantis-simis no- | stri temporis Symphoniacis, continen- | tur: quæ in sacris catholicorum templis | festis sanctorum diebus cantantur, atque | & ad quæ vis instrumenta musica accom- | modatae sunt: Petri Ioannelli de Gandino | Bergomensis summo studio ac labore | collectæ, eiusq; expensis impressæ. | Venetijs Apud Antonium Gar-danum. | 1568 | CUM GRAT: ET PRIVIL: | Sac: Ro: Cae: Ma: Et Ill: Senatus Venet:

These two volumes of Gardano's *Novus Thesaurus Musicus* contain seven Lasso motets, of which two are undisputed first editions: "Audi, benigne conditor," no. 27 in RISM 1568[2] and no. 22 in this volume, and "Domine, quando veneris (2)," no. 49 in RISM 1568[4] and no. 23 in this volume. One other, "In monte Oliveti," was published simultaneously in RISM 1568a and 1568[2] and appears in *CM 6*. As usual in Gardano's editions, the text of both motets is error free. A full description of these sources and a list of their contents may be found in Åke Davidsson, *Catalogue critique et descriptif des imprimés de musique des xvie et xviie siècles conservés a la Bibliothèque de l'Université Royale d'Upsala*, vol. 3, *Receuils de musique religieuse et profane* (Upsala: n.p., 1951), 60–65. I used a microfilm of the copies held by the Bayerische Staatsbibliothek, Munich.

RISM 1569[8]: LIBER SECVNDVS | SACRARVM CAN-TIONVM QVA- | TUOR VOCVM, (VVLGO MOTETAS VOCANT) | CANTVI, OMNISQVE GENERIS INSTRV-MENTIS | *accommodatarum, summa diligentia editus.* | Auc-toribus. | ORLANDO DI LASSUS. | CYPRIANO DE RORE. | *CONTRATENOR.* | LOVANII | Excudebat Petrus Phalesius Typographus Iuratus. Anno 1569.

There are four partbooks: superius, contratenor, tenor and bassus. I used a microfilm of the sole surviv-ing complete copy held by the Biblioteka Gdańska Pol-skiej Akademii Nauk, Gdańska. It is the earliest known source for three motets by Lasso, nos. 24–26 in this vol-ume: "Tribulationem et dolorem inveni," "Laetentur caeli," and "Fratres, sobrii estote." The texts of all three are nearly error free. The contents of the source are:

[Motets by Lasso:]
1. Domine quando veneris
2. Audi dulcis amica mea
3. Inclina Domine aurem tuam

4. Tribulationem et dolorem; 2.p. Convertere animam
5. Laetentur cœli; 2.p. Tunc exultebant
6. Fratres, sobrii estote
7. Fertur in conviviis
8. Quis mihi hoc tribuat; 2.p. Vocabis me et ego
9. Quia vidisti me, Thoma

[Motets by Rore:]
10. O crux benedicta
11. Beati omnes (2 partes)
12. Stetit Jesus (2 partes)
13. Deus pacis
14. Sub tuum praesidium

RISM 1570d: MELLANGE | D'ORLANDE DE LASSVS, | CONTENANT PLVSIEVRS CHANSONS, | TANT EN VERS LATINS QV'EN | RYME FRANCOYSE. | A QVA-TRE, CINQ, SIX, HVIT, DIX, PARTIES. | A PARIS. | *Par Adrian le Roy & Robert Ballard,* | *Imprimeurs du Roy.* | 1570. | Auec priuilege de sa majesté.

A full description and list of contents of this source may be found in Lesure and Thibault, *Bibliographie,* 139–41. I used the complete copy held by the Bayerische Staatsbibliothek, Munich. As mentioned above, this is the earliest printed source for no. 7 in this volume, "Dulces exuviae," as well as other motets that will appear in *CM 18.* It includes several other motets printed in this volume, but it has not been consulted for them.

RISM 1573i: *SUPERIUS.* | DIXHVICTIEME LIVRE. | DE CHANSONS A QVATRE | & à cinq parties par Orlande de lassus, | Imprimé en quatre volumes. | A PARIS. | Par Adrian le Roy, & Robert Ballard, Imprimeurs | du Roy. | 1573. | Auec priuilege de sa maiesté | Pour dix ans.

A full description of this source may be found in Lesure and Thibault, *Bibliographie,* 167, no. 181. Its contents are the same as RISM 1565f. Since the superius partbook of the latter is missing, this source was used to supply that voice for "Deus qui bonum vinum creasti," no. 15 in this volume. I used a microfilm of the only surviving copy of this partbook held by the Bibliothèque Royale, Brussels.

RISM 1576i: SVPERIVS [CONTRA, TENOR, BASSVS, QVINTA ET SEXTA PARS] | LES MESLANGES | D'OR-LANDE DE LASSVS. | CONTENANTZ | PLVSIEVRS CHANSONS, | A IIII, V, VI, VIII, X, PARTIES: | REVEVS PAR LVY, ET AVGMENTEZ. | A PARIS. | Par Adrian le Roy, & Robert Ballard. | Imprimeurs du Roy. | M. V. LXXVI. | Auec priuilege de sa majesté.

A full description of this source may be found in *CM 6,* 202; contents are listed in Lesure and Thibault, *Bibliographie,* 179–80. It has been used in this volume to verify and correct readings from earlier sources.

RISM 1579a: SELECTISSIMÆ CAN- | TIONES, QVAS VVLGO MOTETAS UO- | CANT, PARTIM OMNINO NOVÆ, PARTIM NVSQVAM IN | *Germania excusæ, Sex &*

pluribus vocibus compositæ, per excel- | *lentißimum Musicum* | *ORLANDVM DI LASSVS.* | Posteriori huic editioni accessêre omnes Orlandi Motetæ, quæ in veteri no- | stro Thesauro Musico impressæ continebantur, cum quibusdam alijs, ita vt ferè tertia parte opus hoc sit auctius. *Omnia denuò multò quàm antehac correctius edita.* | DIS-CANTVS [ALTVS, TENOR, BASSVS, QVINTA VOX, SEXTA VOX] | *NORIBERGÆ,* | Imprimebatur in officina typographica Catharinæ Ger- | lachin, & Hæredum Iohannis Montani. | M. D. LXXIX.

RISM 1579b: ALTERA PARS | SELECTISSIMARVM | CANTIONVM, QVAS VVLGO MOTETAS VO- | CANT, QVINQVE ET QVATVOR VOCIBVS COM- | POSI-TARVM PER EXCELLENTISSI- | MVM MVSICVM, | *ORLANDVM DI LASSVS,* | Aucta & restituta, vt suprà indicavimus. | DISCANTVS [ALTVS, TENOR, BASSVS, QVINTA VOX] | NORIBERGÆ, | Imprimebatur in officina typographica Catharina Ger- | lachin, & Hæredum Iohannis Montani, | M. D. LXXIX.

A full description and list of contents of these sources may be found in *CM 6.* They have been used in this volume to verify and correct readings from earlier sources.

Editorial Methods

The following editorial methods are used in all volumes of this series:

1. The original note values are used, that is, transcription at the ratio 1:1, including passages in coloration. The last note in the last measure of a motet or one of its *partes* is transcribed as a brevis with fermata, regardless of its appearance in the source, unless it arrives after a measure begins, in which case it is transcribed as a value sufficient to fill the measure and also provided with a fermata.

2. Barlines are inserted through each staff of the score after each brevis. Double barlines are used to delineate *partes* and changes in meter. The measures are numbered continuously through all *partes* of motets in more than one *pars.*

3. Compositions with the signature ₵ are transcribed in $\frac{4}{2}$ meter. Proportional signatures that indicate triple meter or division, such as φ or $\frac{3}{2}$, are represented by their modern equivalents. Whenever the signature changes within a piece, the original signatures are also shown above the uppermost staff of the score, with equivalence indicated (e.g., o = ⋈·).

4. Notes that continue past a barline in the transcription are divided into appropriate values and connected with a tie. Eighth and sixteenth notes in the transcription are joined with a beam where possible, up to a maximum of four.

5. Ligatures and coloration in the original are shown by full and open brackets, respectively. Coloration that causes triplets is also shown either by (a) the

numeral 3, whether or not it appears in the original; or (b) a change of meter, in which case equivalence will be indicated. When triplets are in values larger than eighths, that is, without beams, a bracket with the numeral 3 from the first and last notes of the triplet figure is added.

6. The original clef, signature, mensuration sign, first note, and any preceding rests in each voice part are shown in an incipit at the beginning of each motet before the brace. The range of each voice is shown after the modern clef, showing pitches as they appear in the modern clefs. When a voice is added after the first part of a motet, it uses the same original clef and moves within the range indicated for the part with which it is paired (cantus 1 and cantus 2, etc.). Exceptions are detailed in the critical notes.

7. Designation of voice parts is normalized to cantus, altus, tenor, and bassus (C, A, T, B), with original designations other than these indicated in the critical notes. Voice parts originally designated quinta vox, sexta vox, etc., are designated cantus 2, altus 2, tenor 2, bassus 2, or the like, according to their clef and range. The original designations of these parts are indicated in the source section.

8. Without regard to the designation of a voice part, (a) parts originally in any G clef or C1 or C2 (C on the first or second line respectively) are transcribed in the treble clef; (b) parts originally in C3 or C4 clefs are transcribed in transposed treble clef; and (c) parts originally in C5 or any F clef are transcribed in bass clef.

9. Accidentals on the staff appear in the principal or concordant source and have their normal meanings in modern practice. All original accidentals have been retained, including those that are redundant or unnecessary in modern practice. The original sign ✕ is transcribed as ♯ or ♮ depending on context, with no further indication in the critical notes. Accidentals on the staff that appear in brackets have been added by the editor when repetitions of the same pitch extend over a barline in the transcription and only the first note in the series has an accidental in the original. If an original or bracketed accidental on the staff is no longer valid when the same pitch is repeated later in the same measure, it is canceled with a bracketed sign when the source does not indicate cancellation. Cautionary accidentals are not normally supplied; Lasso's style includes frequent successive cross-relations, and to supply cautionaries for all of these would clutter the page unduly.

All other accidentals added by the editor are shown above the staff in small type. These accidentals are *not* to be understood as optional; the editors consider them obligatory in accordance with conventions of Lasso's time. These conventions include (a) raised leading tones at cadences; (b) accidentals that correct successive or simultaneous diminished or augmented fourths, fifths, or octaves; (c) accidentals that follow the principle of *nota super la*, that is, that prevent a melodic tritone when a voice ascends above *la* in the prevailing hexachord; (d) accidentals that achieve progression to a perfect consonance from the nearest imperfect consonance. Accidentals above the staff are valid only for the note over which they appear; they are repeated within a measure whenever necessary.

10. The motets in the present edition are placed in chronological order according to the earliest source (preferably the earliest printed source) for each and then numbered consecutively through the volume. The titles are supplied from the indexes of the sources, with orthography and punctuation adjusted as necessary. The sources used for each motet are indicated in the individual discussions below, with comments in the critical notes always referring to the source named first unless otherwise indicated. Abbreviations in the original text are expanded without comment unless they are in some way questionable or unclear, and the distinctions between *i j* and *u v* have been normalized in accordance with the sources mentioned. Repetitions of text shown in the original by an idem sign (*ij, %,* etc.) are enclosed in angle brackets in the edition. Editorial additions of text are enclosed in square brackets. If it is necessary to show the original orthography, this is done in "Texts and Translations," or alternately in the critical notes. Text underlay follows that of the principal source unless otherwise indicated in the critical notes.

Critical Notes

The notes report all textual and musical differences between the sources and the edition that are not covered by stated editorial principles. The notes give the number of each motet in the *Magnum Opus Musicum*. This numeration is identical to that in *SW* (but not its concurrent numeration of subsidiary *partes* in motets of two or more movements). The following abbreviations are employed in the notes: M(m). = measure(s), C = cantus, C 1 = cantus primus, C 2 = cantus secundus, A = altus, A 1 = altus primus, A 2 = altus secundus, T = tenor, T 1 = tenor primus, T 2 = tenor secundus, B = bassus, B 1 = bassus primus, B 2 = bassus secundus. Pitches are given according to the system in which middle C is c'.

1. Audi dulcis amica mea
No. 60 in *MOM*
Source: RISM 1555b.

2. Peccantem me quotidie
No. 90 in *MOM*
Source: RISM 1555b.

3. Inclina Domine aurem tuam
No. 104 in *MOM*

Source: RISM 1555b.
M. 59, C, note 3, underlay is "tu-."

4. *Domine, quando veneris (1)*

No. 144 in *MOM*
Source: RISM 1555b.

5. *Alma Nemes*

No. 138 in *MOM* (contrafactum)
Source: RISM 1555b.

6. *Calami sonum ferentes*

MOM deest
Source: RISM 1555b.

Mm. 6–15, all voices, underlay is "levem" rather than "leve." Mm. 29–30, underlay is "constrepente" rather than "qui strepente." M. 40, T, note 2 is brevis followed by semibrevis and brevis rests, with mensuration change at m. 43. M. 41, C, mensuration changes at m. 43; A, mensuration changes at m. 42.

7. *Dulces exuviae*

No. 305 in *MOM*
Primary source: Mu 20; concordant source: RISM 1570d.

Layout in Mu 20: C, B on verso, A, T 2, T 1 on recto; in *secunda pars* C 1, C 2, B on verso and A, T 2, T 1 on recto; no voice parts are named.

In RISM 1570d T 2 and C 2 in quinta pars partbook.
M. 10, A, Mu 20, diesis appears only before note 3. M. 12, C, Mu 20, note 1 lacks flat. M. 19, B, 1570d, note 2 lacks diesis. M. 35, T 2, Mu 20, three semibreves; underlay is "fortuna." M. 36, T 2, Mu 20, notes 1–2, underlay is "pere-." M. 49, A, T 1, T 2, Mu 20, underlay "et" added in another hand (Lasso's?). M. 59, C 2 has C-clef on first line in both sources; its range does not exceed that of C 1. M. 80, T 1, Mu 20, diesis precedes note 2, not note 1. M. 81, T 2, Mu 20, note 2 is d. M. 82, C 2, Mu 20, note 1 lacks diesis. Mm. 86–89, Mu 20, repetitions of "felix" frequently omitted, with some added in another hand (Lasso's?). M. 88, C 2, Mu 20, note 2 lacks diesis. M. 113, B, Mu 20, notated originally as two semibreves, corrected with a tie. M. 114, C 2, 1570b, note 2 lacks diesis. Mm. 114–17, B, Mu 20, underlay is "et impressa," corrected with line from "et" to m. 113, note 1, and "toro" added in mm. 116–17. Mm. 118–21, all voices, Mu 20, underlay is "moriamur inultum" with correction to "moriemur inultae." M. 120, note 2, to m. 122, note 2, C 1, C 2, and A, Mu 20, underlay lacking. M. 133, note 4, to m. 134, note 1, T 2, Mu 20, two minims (page break) with "-um-" under m. 134, note 1. M. 152, C 1, Mu 20, note 1 lacks diesis.

8. *Alma Venus*

No. 170 in *MOM* (contrafactum)

Primary source: RISM 1560b; concordant source: RISM 1576i.

In RISM 1560b T 2 in quinta pars partbook.
M. 2, A, note 3, underlay is "-nus." M. 6, B, note 5, underlay is "-to." M. 15, T 2, note 1, underlay is "nus." M. 20, all voices, brevis with fermata. M. 47, T 2, note 2, minim and semiminim b♭, emendation from 1576i. Mm. 103–4, C, A, and T 1, underlay is "ocula" rather than "oculis." M. 114 to end, A, T 1, B, the underlay of 1576i is added beneath that of RISM 1560b.

9. *Tityre, tu patulae*

No. 473 in *MOM*
Primary sources: RISM 1560b for *prima pars*, RISM 1568a for secunda pars; concordant sources: RISM 1568a, RISM 1576i, RISM 1579a.

In RISM 1560b, 1568a, and 1579a C 2 in quinta pars partbook, B 1 in sexta pars partbook; in RISM 1576i C 2 and B 1 in quinta et sexta pars partbook.

The earliest sources for this motet print only its first part. These sources include four reprints of RISM 1560b (RISM 1562c, 1566h, 1570f, and 1573f) and two issues of Le Roy and Ballard's *Quatorsiesme livre de chansons* (RISM 1561[6] and 1564[10]). RISM 1568a is the earliest known source for the second part and is used as its primary source in this edition. 1568a is also used to emend the faulty text of 1560b, and 1576i is used for the same purpose, representing the later Le Roy and Ballard prints that include both parts of the motet. A few variants are reported from 1579a. Unless otherwise indicated, corrections of 1560b in the first part are derived from both 1568a and 1576i, in which the texts are nearly identical. The source of each correction of 1568a in the second part is reported separately.

Prima pars. M. 1, A, 1579a, note 3 is f♯'. Mm. 13–14, all voices, 1560b, underlay is "avaena." M. 15, A, 1560b, 1568a, and 1576i, note 2 is e', corrected in 1579a. M. 16, A, 1560b, note 1 replaced by minim e', minim d'. M. 17, note 2, to m. 21, note 1, C 1, 1560b, underlay is "et dulcia linquimus arva." M. 19, T 1, 1560b, note 2 is g. Mm. 20–26, T, 1560b, as shown in example 1.

M. 21, note 2, to m. 26, note 3, C 1, *ij.* M. 21, C 2, 1560b, note 3 is minim rest and minim c♯"; A, 1560b, note 3 is f'. M. 22, B 1, 1560b, note 3 is g. M. 26, B 1, 1560b, note 1 replaced by minim a, minim a. M. 34, T, 1560b, note 2 is g, changed by hand to e in Kassel copy (1568a, 1576i, and 1579a have a). M. 37, A, 1579a, note 1 is c♯'. M. 37, note 3, to m. 38, note 1, A, 1560b, no ligature (connected by hand in Kassel copy). M. 48, note 1, to m. 51, note 1, C 2, 1560b, ij. M. 51, note 2, to m. 55, note 2, C 2, underlay is "re-sonare doces Amarillida silvas" (this edition follows 1579a, which differs slightly from 1568a and 1576i [c.f., C 1, mm. 38–47]).

Secunda pars. M. 97, C 1, 1568a and 1576i, note 4 is d", correction from 1579a. M. 100, A, and 107, A, 1568a and 1576i, note 2 is d', correction from 1579a. M. 109, note 2, to m. 110, note 1, T, 1568a, ligature f–g, correction from 1576i and 1579a; B 2, 1568a, ligature G–A, correction from 1576i and 1579a.

10. *Quia vidisti me, Thoma*

No. 78 in *MOM*
Primary source: RISM 1563³; concordant sources: RISM 1566f and 1568b.

The underlay in RISM 1566f and 1568b diverges several times from that of RISM 1563³. These variants are not reported here.

M. 2, A, 1566f and 1568b, note 1 is c♯'. M. 3, C, 1566f and 1568b, note 3 is g♯'.

11. *Scio enim quod redemptor meus vivit*

No. 143 in *MOM*
Source: RISM 1563³.
M. 20, A, rest is brevis.

12. *Fertur in conviviis*

No. 141 in *MOM* (contrafactum)
Primary source: RISM 1564d; concordant sources: RISM 1576i and 1579b. In 1576l, 1579b, and some other sources, the five sections of this motet, each of which ends with a fermata, are designated "partes."

M. 4, B, note 1 is e. M. 9, A, note 3 is missing. M. 17, note 1, to m. 18, note 2, all voices, longa, brevis, longa, brevis, longa, brevis; this edition's usual practice of retaining the original note values would be misleading here. Lasso normally notated a passage like this in filled semibreves and minims, which is in fact how it appears in other sources, including 1576i and 1579b. M. 41, A, note 3, dot missing. Mm. 44–45, all voices, longa, brevis, longa, brevis, longa, brevis; see the note for mm. 17–18 (however, 1576i and 1579b change the signature here to ₵3). M. 57, note 2, to m. 61, note 2, all voices, longa, brevis, longa, brevis, longa, brevis, dotted longa, longa, brevis, longa, brevis, longa, brevis, longa, brevis; see the note for mm. 17–18 (1576i and 1579b, m. 59, note 1 is void). M. 68, C, note 4 is e". M. 93, B, note 3 is a. M. 97, B, note 1 is f. M. 100, T, underlay is "-tes pro e-." M.

101, T, note 1, underlay is "bri-;" note 4, underlay is "-is" (mm. 100–101 corrected from 1576i).

13. *Quid prodest stulto*

No. 221 in *MOM*
Primary source: RISM 1566c; concordant sources: RISM 1564d and 1565c. Placement of the text in 1564d is notably inferior to that of the Italian sources, especially 1566c. Variants in 1564d are reported except for *ij* signs that agree with the underlay in 1566c, since 1566c writes out all text repetitions fully.

M. 3, note 3, to m. 6, note 1, A, 1564d, underlay is "stulto habere divitias." M. 6, note 2, to m. 7, note 1, A, 1564d, *ij*. M. 7, A, 1564d, notes 2–3, underlay is "habe-." M. 12, C, 1564d, notes 2 and 3 are combined into a single semibrevis; underlay for the measure is "-pienti-." M. 15, note 3, to m. 16, note 3, C, 1564d, underlay is "emere non pos-". M. 16, C, 1564d, notes 3 and 4 are combined into one semibrevis; A, 1564d, note 6 is undotted minim. M. 17, A, 1564d, note 1 is not tied, underlay is "pos-." M. 18, C, 1564d, note 2 is dotted minim (tied over the barline); syllable "al-" under note 5 of m. 19. M. 20, C, 1564d, note 5 is g'. M. 23, T 1, 1564d, note 3 is g'. M. 37, A, 1564d, notes 1–3 are dotted minim and two fusas. M. 42, C, 1564d, note 1 lacks diesis.

14. *Pater, peccavi*

No. 217 in *MOM*
Primary source: RISM 1564d; concordant sources: Mu 20, RISM 1565a, and 1568b. As in no. 13, the underlay in 1564d is sometimes faulty. It has been emended from 1565a (1568b for C 2), but 1564d is still taken as the primary source, since its flaws are less substantial in no. 14 than in no. 13. Differences in the placement of *ij* in the two later printed sources are not reported. The underlay given in Mu 20 agrees with 1565a and 1568b except as noted below. The *ij* sign is almost completely lacking in Mu 20, and differences in its placement are also not reported. Differences among the sources in the use of minor color instead of dotted notes are not reported.

In RISM 1564d C 2 in quinta pars partbook; in 1565a and 1568b C 1 in quinta vox partbook. Layout in Mu 20: C 1, C 2, and B on verso, A and T on recto; no voice parts are named.

M. 9, note 2, to m. 11, note 2, T, 1564d, underlay is "peccavi, *ij*." M. 11, note 3, to m. 15, note 1, A, 1564d, *ij*. M. 12, note 1, to m. 14, note 3, T, 1564d, underlay is "in caelum et coram te, *ij*." M. 13, note 1, to m. 14, note 3, C 1, 1564d, underlay is "et coram te, *ij*," with no text given until m. 18. M. 15, A, 1564d, note 2, *ij*. M. 28, C 2, 1564d, note 2, *ij*, with no text given until m. 38, note 2. M. 29, A, 1564d, notes 2–4, underlay is "tuus, *ij*," with no text given until m. 33. M. 39, C 2, 1568b and Mu 20, note 2 lacks diesis. M. 43, A, note 4 has diesis only in 1564d.   M. 48, A, 1564d, note 2, underlay is "tu-."   M. 49, A, 1564d, note 3 is b♭.   M. 66, C 2, 1564d, note 3, underlay is "-is"; A, 1564b, note 1, *ij*, with no text given to the end of *prima pars*.   M. 69, T, Mu 20, note 3 omitted.   M. 89, C 1, Mu 20, note 4, underlay is "me-."   M. 91, C 1, 1565a, note 2 lacks diesis.   M. 115, C 2, 1564d, note 2, *ij*, with no text given until m. 122, note 3.   M. 120, note 2, to m. 123, note 2, A, 1564d, underlay is "et dicam ei, *ij*," with no text given until m. 130, note 2.   M. 122, T, 1564d, note 1, *ij*.   M. 135, T, note 4, diesis appears only in 1564d. M. 137, note 2, diesis appears only in 1564d.   M. 140, note 2, to m. 144, note 1, A, 1564d, underlay is "tuis, *ij*," adjusted to agree with mm. 48–49.   M. 143, note 2, to m. 144, note 5, A, 1564d, semibrevis c′ and minim b, adjusted to agree with mm. 51–52.   M. 149, C 1, notes 2–6, 1564d, semibrevis g′ and minim f′, adjusted to agree with C 2, m. 57.   M. 160, note 4, to m. 161, note 2, A, 1564d, underlay is "tuis *ij*."   M. 161, C 2, 1564d, note 1 is two semibreves f′-f′.

15. Deus qui bonum vinum creasti

No. 140 in *MOM* (contrafactum)
Sources: RISM 1565f (A, T, B) and 1573i (C).

16. Forte soporifera

No. 315 in *MOM* (contrafactum)
Primary source: RISM 1566[17]; concordant source: RISM 1579b.

M. 43, note 3, to m. 44, note 4, and m. 49, note 3, to m. 50, note 4, A, underlay is "curatur nullis," emended from 1579b.   M. 49, note 3, to m. 50, note 4, C, underlay is "curator nullis," emended to agree with mm. 43–44.

17. Quis est homo qui timet Dominum?

No. 264 in *MOM*
Source: RISM 1568b.
In RISM 1568b T 2 in quinta vox partbook.
M. 30, A, note 4 is b.

18. Ubi est Abel

No. 231 in *MOM*
Source: RISM 1568b.
In RISM 1568b A 2 in quinta vox partbook.
M. 16, S, A, T, underlay is "dicit" rather than "dixit."   M. 19, all voices, longa followed by a single barline.   M. 37, B, note 1, underlay is "e-."

19. Quem dicunt homines

No. 213 in *MOM*
Source: RISM 1568b.
In RISM 1568b T 2 in quinta vox partbook.
M. 42, C, note 1 is e″.   M. 48, B, note 2 is g.   M. 66, C, note 3 is minim.

20. Jesu, nostra redemptio

No. 339 in *MOM*
Source: RISM 1568a.
In RISM 1568a A 2 in sexta vox partbook, B 2 in quinta vox partbook.
M. 91, A 2, underlay is "nostro."

21. S, U, su, P, E, R, per

No. 280 in *MOM*
Sources: RISM 1567[13] (C, A 1, A 2, B) and RISM 1570[14] (T).
In RISM 1567[13] A 2 in quinto partbook.
M. 41, A 1, note 1 is c′.

22. Audi, benigne conditor

No. 233 in *MOM*
Source: RISM 1568[2].
In RISM 1568[2] B 2 in quintus partbook.

23. Domine, quando veneris (2)

MOM deest
Source: RISM 1568[4].
In RISM 1568[4] T 2 in quintus partbook.

24. Tribulationem et dolorem inveni

No. 94 in *MOM*
Source: RISM 1569[8].
M. 55, T, note 3 is d′.   M. 100, B, note 1 is B♭.

25. Laetentur caeli

No. 127 in *MOM*
Source: RISM 1569[8].
M. 58, B, note 5, underlay is "ve-."

26. Fratres, sobrii estote

No. 73 in *MOM*
Source: RISM 1569[8].
M. 12, C, A, T, brevis with fermata; B, *cum opposita proprietate* ligature with fermata.   M. 39, B, note 1 is c.

RECENT RESEARCHES IN THE MUSIC OF THE RENAISSANCE
James Haar, general editor